ALL JOIN HANDS

ALL JOIN HANDS

Dudley Laufman
& the New England Country Dance Tradition

Thomas S. Curren

Peter E. Randall Publisher
Portsmouth, New Hampshire
2023

Other books by Tom Curren

A Bicentennial History of Bridgewater, N.H.

A Small Town by the River (Northfield, N.H.)

History of New Hampton, N.H. (with Kathy Neustadt)

Home to the Mountain (Wilmot, N.H.) (with Kathy Neustadt)

I Believe I'll Go Back Home:
Roots and Revival in New England Folk Music

© 2023 by Thomas S. Curren
All rights reserved in all media.

ISBN 13: 978-1-942155-55-3
Library of Congress Control Number: 2022919737

Produced by Peter E. Randall Publisher
5 Greenleaf Woods Drive, Suite 102
Portsmouth, NH 03801
www.perpublisher.com

Cover design by Tim Holtz
Cover photo by Steve Booth; cover art by Pieter Bruegel the Elder

Unless otherwise noted, photographs courtesy of Dudley Laufman

Printed in the United States of America

Contents

Introduction

THE DRIVEWAY TO DUDLEY LAUFMAN'S PLACE is a quick right-hand turn through the green wood; his homemade house is set back behind a growth of ambitious young maples and one vigorous old pear tree. Even before the leaves come out, it is easy to overshoot the turn and to find yourself passing by the eloquent single stone in the nearby Shaker cemetery. On a soft and overcast April morning, you can walk along a stone wall by a lavender crocus bed and scare a few purple finches and a downy woodpecker away from the bird feeder. "Come in!" is the answer to a knock on the door, followed by "You want a cup of coffee?" I'm usually pretty well coffee'd up by mid-morning, so I say no, thanks, and take a seat at the kitchen table. "How you doing?" I ask. "Pretty good," says Dudley. "I was going to plant some peas, but it was still pretty damp this morning and my hips are a little stiff. You?" "Oh, I'm good. Did you get a chance to read the manuscript?" "I did," he says. "I liked it. Top drawer stuff. Except there's nothing in here about my time in Hillsborough, but that's OK, I haven't told you about that yet. It's all in this notebook." He slides a worn, blue, three-ring binder across the table top. "Be careful with it," he says. "Will do. Anything else?" "I liked your mention of Clement Weeks, the old dancer from the Seacoast," he says. "Where did you run across him?" "That was in an article by Kate Van Winkle Keller in that big Colonial Society book.

She talks about his tune book from 1783. How do you know him?" "I wrote a poem about him five years ago. It's in here." And he goes to the shelf and hands me a volume I hadn't seen before entitled *This Is The Day We've Been Waiting For*.

"We're gaining on this, Dudley," I say. He nods: "I know it." "But we've gotta clip along here. Time to get the gardens in soon. This is going to be a busy summer for both of us." So I flip open the yellow legal pad in its leather folder, and we plow on into the story like a small-town highway crew working on a dirt road, filling in the dips, picking the rocks up, leaving the public way crowned and ditched so as to get from one place to another. A couple of hours later, we finish up for the day: I've got to go catch a Zoom call and he's got an appointment with a chiropractor. "You OK for next Friday?" He checks the calendar on the wall. "Sure am." "All right, then, see you in the forenoon!" He walks me to the door, past a glowing red diamond pane in a window that he glazed in 1959. "We covered a lot of good ground today." He pauses. "Are you going to write about me being ninety-one now, and things slowing down some?" "Yeah, I will, but I heard you get two gigs today on the phone." "I used to have dozens of them." "Well, it's only April, and there's still the Covid, you know." "Can you put something in the book about Nanci, how she knows all my tunes and hums along in harmony in her car?" "I will, Dudley. Please give her my best." "OK. You drive careful," he says. "I will! You, too! Take care. See you Friday." I drive past the old pear tree. It looks like it might be budding up for the bees by next week. We'll see.

This is a story about what happened when a ten-thousand-year-old musical tradition put itself into the hands of a seventeen-year-old Boston boy in 1947.

Before the data chip and the dirigible, before indoor plumbing, and before the invention of title and entitlement, our human cultures developed through eons of daily experience and folk tradition. Only in the more recent centuries have we become accustomed to overlooking the community influences that give human dimension to the verb "to be." Organized civilization has trained us to focus our history and our self-identification in terms of status, politics, war, wealth, fashion, and fame. We are firmly acculturated to see the course of human events through filters that are long on conditioned assumptions and short on perspective, inspiration, or faith. We aren't all that good at practicing "the humanities" right now. Despite our "tough guy" exteriors, we seem to have softened more than a bit at the core. Perhaps we should not be surprised when, even as we revel in drive-thru ease, we experience the nagging feeling that we have no idea what the hell we are doing.

We're having to cope with frightening factors of the sort that we have long been led to believe we were exempt from. Perhaps such things have always been lurking just beneath the surfaces of our understanding, and now they have simply asserted themselves into our brief attention spans in the manner of a long-deferred balloon payment or a demand note. We may be well served by taking a good look back at the cultural tools that humans have used to survive and endure when we had daily reason to depend upon and to be dependable to our neighbors. The importance of contributing to part of a "social network" predates the invention of the computer by thousands of years. In living memory, our human community pitches in and does a lot of its best work when the electricity fails.

We have been conditioned to think mechanistically for well more than a century now, but the shift away from the personal and community aspects of the human nature began with the rise of the city-state long, long ago. Civilized power tended to dilute and then eradicate ancient forms of creative communal expression. By the time that the Reformation took hold in Europe in the 1500s, many of the old ways were being branded as Satanic and people who engaged in traditional forms of celebration or ribaldry (not to mention the folk arts of midwifery, herbal medicine, and astrology) might find themselves tied to a stake and surrounded by kindling. In "civilized" countries, thousands of people were put to death over fine points of religious belief. The situation became so dire in some cases that emigration to a perilous new world seemed to be the most viable alternative.

And so, in the seventeenth century, hopeful immigrants to North America began to intrude upon Native cultures that were already perhaps as much as ten thousand years old. As humans often do, these newcomers began to confuse their conditioned assumptions, their fears, and their ambitions with the truths that others had already long established on the ground. Thousands of souls were living here before any sort of Europeans arrived, and the evidence points us toward the conclusion that the Native peoples had figured out how to live in balance with the natural world around them.

Civilized "special interests" have long sought to impose their imperatives upon the Americas, Africa, Asia, Australia, and now even the neighboring planets. Not a lot of thought has gone into "progress" ahead of time, other than to respond to the impulses to establish control, to fill entitled pockets, and to maintain full speed ahead. Although much separates the experiences of North American, European, African, and other folk cultures in this saga, by now we may well share in the feeling that, over time, *we've all been had*. Modern westerners would do well to come to an understanding of how deeply the forgotten ways of their Anglo-European village ancestors have been beguiled by the pride and betrayed by the prejudice of Empire. There is much to remember, there is much for us to learn how to learn, and there is much need of healing.

By the close of the nineteenth century, the Industrial Age had driven rural culture off the cliffs of finance, function, and fashion. After people needed to have cash to survive, they were required to go to where the money was (the city) and to do what the city wanted done (through a job based upon the marketability of gender, race, class, status, and conditioning). In modern culture, anything that is not novel, commercial, and fashionable *does not really seem to exist*, and certainly doesn't *count*. Permanence and stability have receded in importance; there need not be much distance anymore in between invention, cash-out, and extinction. We pay little heed to consequences till they have us by the throat.

We seem to have spent much of the course of the last hundred years, at least, engaged in the complicated act of painting ourselves into a sophisticated corner. Countless advances in material life can be celebrated as miracles, but in the sum total of our daily existence, it is difficult to feel now that we are really making a lot of forward progress as human beings. We have ingested so many modern cultural antibiotics that our creative and our intuitive innards don't function the way that they ought to. Overfed yet undernourished, we spend a lot of time dealing with a bellyache, either our own or somebody else's.

As relentless as this process has been, it has not gone unchallenged. Vigorous American voices have championed heritage, freedom, and creativity as salvational counterbalances to all the *diabolus ex machinae* in our lives. At least since the Revolution and its succeeding reform movements, there has been a growing understanding that we overlook our cultural health at our collective peril. Something there is that doesn't love a modern wall, that pulls it down and allows the integrity of old tunes, revivals, heirloom vegetables, juke joints, post and beam construction, good rowboats, and single malt Scotch to jump the fences and flourish in free range.

In no way has this been more evident than in the revivals of traditional music. The folk and roots music rebirths of the twentieth century allowed blues, bluegrass, ballads, ragtime, poetic recital, and country music to come back to life and, in the case of rock 'n' roll, to bring us together across our long-festering racial divides. Music has been a dependable oasis in the long, parched journey towards community that first united us as American pilgrims. The Boston-Cambridge Folk Revival (and its fellow lonesome travelers throughout the country) acted as a force for diversity in a world that has been subjugated to the dictates of cultural algorithm since the 1950s. The emotional power of traditional music has been a saving grace in the face of many of our excesses and most of our deficits. Long ago, someone should have given a Grammy Award to Grandma.

And so we come to the subject of traditional country dance, and to its role to act as one expression of our basic humanity. Dance lifts us bodily out of our inhibitions, our anxieties, and our acculturated need to exert control. It requires our participation as individuals, yet it is experienced as an exercise in group dynamic. The case could be made that country dance has survived in a purer form than some other traditional arts and crafts, since dance usually lends itself only to commerce at the level of the passing of a hat. As the *Christian Science Monitor* once noted in an article on Dudley Laufman, "The essence of the dance lies in the fact that it is a non-competitive activity, one in which it is nearly impossible to remain self-centered."[1]

A number of factors would have seemed to decrease the odds for the survival of American country dance in the modern era, but the form has had a few very good things going for it. First and foremost, the traditional tunes are beautiful. In order to give every couple in the set time enough to complete their steps, the music reprises, ebbing and flowing in waves that may, at first, sound repetitive to the modern ear but that a good group of musicians enlivens with subtleties of rhythm, tone, volume, and emphasis that become both mesmeric and exciting.

Second, and possibly less examined, is the role of physical contact that is central to the country dance experience. On the one hand, a YouTube viewing of a traditional dance of any sort is not likely to be seen as a display of libido; some dances are joyful and energetic, but others seem sedate almost to the point of somnambulance, particularly if the participants are wearing snow-tire sandals and wool socks. On the other hand, everyone in the hall touches everybody else in the course of the dance, sometimes in handclasps, sometimes with an arm around a waist, and sometimes in an energetic fling. All this has the potential for a certain mixture of joy, exercise, and excitement, things that are often in cultural short supply in the modern era. Under the right circumstances, a good night at a country dance carries with it the potential to feel like the preface to romance. If a fading picture of staid old Ralph Page

---

1. *The Christian Science Monitor*, Arts & Entertainment section, September 19, 1973.

dancing with a lithe, smiling woman who is wearing a swirling print dress looks appealing, well, maybe there's hope for us all.

There's a third important factor at work here, something akin to what Michael Pollan was getting at when he wrote *The Botany of Desire*. Many times, at the last moment before extinction has swallowed up traditional dance, it seems to have attracted or perhaps commandeered some good soul who picks it up, dusts it off, and delivers it from the weevils of fashion. In England, John Playford began writing down country dance tunes around the same time that the Puritans were trying to stomp the form out of existence during the 1600s. Tunes and steps were documented faithfully in rural enclaves on both sides of the pond through the nineteenth and twentieth centuries, and country dancers kept the old ways alive through the daunting throes of the Industrial Revolution and the sleazy glitz of the Gilded Age. In New England, people like to take the measure of themselves in all the old, familiar places. Traditional ways have been entrusted to us in parcels secured with stout threads of affection, of art, and of magic. We take the time to learn how to make quilts, grow pumpkins, sing the blues, and cook on wood stoves. The Yankee instinct for preservation has been a major dynamic behind Dudley Laufman's life-long stewardship of country dance, which is the story and the focus of this book.

I was born about twenty years after Dudley Laufman, and raised north of Boston, about ten miles away from where he was brought up. As a boy, I, too, felt a bit miscast in time and place, and found myself paying attention to tales of the pioneers, sea shanties, and Indian Head pennies. I found a cultural foster home in the Boston-Cambridge Folk Revival of the early 1960s, and then moved to the woods of New Hampshire to complete my service as a conscientious objector. I felt deeply drawn to farm life, met and was tolerated by some generous old-timers, learned to garden and to raise critters, and eventually ran a dairy farm at a modest profit. I helped two wonderful girls raise themselves to confident womanhood. I met

Dudley Laufman in Northfield in 1969, attended his contradances, played at a few of them, and ran into him nearly every March at Roy Hutchinson's sugaring off parties in Canterbury. I married folklorist Kathy Neustadt, and began to see things through her influence and example and to benefit from her tolerance of my practice of folklore without a license.

While working as a conservationist for the Pew Charitable Trusts, I drove nearly fifty thousand miles a year, and behind the wheel of my truck I had the opportunity to listen to a rich variety of traditional music recordings on compact disc. In 2014, I began writing *I Believe I'll Go Back Home,* a history of the Boston-Cambridge Folk Revival, and started volunteering for Folk New England, a non-profit music archive now housed at the Special Collections at the University of Massachusetts in Amherst. In concert with Dudley, Jacqueline Laufman, Jack Sloanaker, and Gerry Putnam, I was able to locate and fund the digitization of dozens of Dudley's old original reel-to-reel contradance tapes, the missing links before and after the pivotal "Blue Album" that the Canterbury Country Dance Orchestra recorded in 1971. I grew to know and love that incredible body of work, some of its antecedents, and much of its progeny. In 2016, donors to Folk New England helped fund the *Welcome Here Again* recordings. Dudley and I kept in touch during the course of a pandemic that suddenly threatened our lives and our activities. This mid-winter, he spoke to me of past attempts at his biography that had never been completed, and we talked about taking another crack at it. His take on the first draft served to spur both of us on. We worked together through the late winter to whittle this story out of the life and times of the music.

I hope that you like this book as much as we have enjoyed putting it all together.

Tom Curren
The Chapman Place
Bridgewater, New Hampshire
June 21, 2022

There are lots of isolated "islands" throughout the United States where certain enterprising ones have rescued the country dances much as they would pluck a fine old handicraft out of near-oblivion… There is much to be said for the fine loyalty of these people… worthy recorders of the tribe's ways, and it is due to them alone that many of our old things are more than mere memories today. That, now, is what the country dance can mean. So we hereby nominate the Country Dance Plan as the first crocus in the recovery of civilization from its self-poisoning.

Ralph Page, 1937

They arrive, spilling into the hall like a tipped over basket of many colored balls of heavy yarn, waving college pennants and starting to unravel, spinning around like a parenthesis. Some go down the center like Slinkies—some turn like a brace & bit, others like a dime on edge.

The fiddler rubs rosin along his bow and a fine dust rises out over the hall. He breaks off small pieces, doling them out to the orchestra like ginger. The prompter drinks his down with one swill of flute water, the piano player tapes hers to the bottom of her sandal, the accordion player holds his between his teeth, the banjo player smiles like Jack Palance, and the flute players pass as they take joy in mercury.

Dudley Laufman, 1972

≡ 1 ≡

Fishermen, Fiddlers, and Pharisees

THE LAY OF THE LAND WE KNOW AS NEW ENGLAND is a stage upon which a long drama of human events has played out over the course of time. At the eastern entrance is the ocean, indented by the harbor mouths of great waterways: the Kennebec, the Saco, the Piscataqua, the Merrimack, the Charles (once called the Quinobequin), the Connecticut, the Housatonic, and the western border of the Hudson. English, French, and Basque fishermen had been venturing into the Gulf of Maine since about the time that Anne Boleyn gave birth to the daughter she named Elizabeth. A thousand years of civilization had fished the seas of Europe barren, until hardly a haddock was left that would not fit easily on a forearm. Brave boats crept warily westward towards Greenland fisheries in the 1500s, searching hither and yon for the old-fashioned catch. Eventually a vessel wandered through fog and ice and blundered onto fertile shoals where in twenty minutes a dory could be filled to the gunnels with gasping cod as long as your leg and twice as big around, at the belly, as a stout man's thigh.

For the better part of the good Queen Bess's life and reign, fat boats trundled back eastward laden with salted fish that found ready sale in England and met with high demand in Catholic Europe. In Lisbon, the profits from cod could be traded for barrels of port that would open the purses and then redden the cheeks of the English

1

nobility. It was not only fish that brought forth the pounds and the pieces of eight, but also a by-catch of beaver pelts, fox skins, and mink furs that tidewater Wabanakis swapped in return for brass fish hooks, filet knives, kettles, and axeheads. Trading camps were set up at Damariscove and off Kittery and Portsmouth at "ye Yles of Sholes." Soon after 1600, a few hardy English souls "wintered over" on those islands, and a bit later on as house guests at Native villages in places "on the main" like Boothbay and Biddeford Pool.

About two weeks before William Shakespeare's thirty-ninth birthday, on April 10, 1603, the trade ships *Speedwell* and *Discoverer* left England loaded with goods to be used in barter with the Native people. Pickaxes, saws, hatchets, hooks, "sizzers," looking glasses, beads, thimbles, and thread were among the goods for barter that were carried by these vessels as they cruised the Gulf of Maine between the mouth of the Penobscot and Cape Cod. They anchored off present-day Plymouth, where the trade was so good that a feast of fish, beans, and peas was prepared, a stringed instrument called a "gitterne" was produced from the ship, and a culturally blended dance of about a hundred Wampanoag and English participants took place along the beach.[2] In southern Maine, a Wabanaki man named Scozway mastered the fiddle and played at fishermen's shindigs[3] where mariners "gulped down their home-brewed beer, repeating endlessly the same repertory of bawdy songs and stories, and intensifying the constant battle of wits until a session of rough railery ended in a fist fight."[4]

The men who crewed these boats and the few hardy women who threw their lots in with them were products of the rough and ready rural village culture that has been referred to with affection as

---

2. Charles Knowles Bolton, *The Real Founders of New England* (Boston: F.W. Faxon, 1929), 8.

3. Louis Pichierri, *Music In New Hampshire 1623–1800* (New York: Columbia University Press, 1960), 18.

4. Charles E. Clark, *The Eastern Frontier* (New York: Alfred Knopf, 1970), 22.

"Merrie Old England."[5] In the ancient countryside, hard work in field and kitchen, on wharf and wherry, was broken up by frequent market days, holidays, and observances that combined religion, folklore, and the passage of the seasons. Music of flute and fiddle was commonplace and country dancing was second nature for a people who had no idea what it meant to be an "audience." Tunes and dance steps were mastered as universally as the art of driving an automobile is today. Nearly everyone loved to dance and couples often found love completing a threesome in their dance. Ballads were memorized and repeated, tales of outlaws and battles were sung, many including a moral like a prize hidden in a bag of candy. "Greensleeves" was first published in 1580; a bit later on, in "The Merrie Wives of Windsor," Shakespeare had old Falstaff proclaim: "Let the sky rain potatoes! Let it thunder to the tune of Greensleeves!"

Hundreds, perhaps thousands, of the ancient tunes were well-known, but almost none of them were written down until the 1600s. Numbers like "Childgrove," "The Shepherd's Wife," and "Haste To The Wedding" were likely much older than that, as was a body of jigs, reels, strathspeys, and hornpipes that were played in all celebrations and seasons. Countless generations of children grew up learning these pieces, toddling to the dance floor like ducklings waddling through the rushes and into the water of the village pond. In old rural culture, the local squire's family would join in celebration along with the common folk, especially during the nearly month-long span of Christmas holidays. "Refined" dance steps from town were stirred in with the raucous swingings and clumpings of rural swains and sweethearts. Morris dances, May-Day romps, reels, harvest gatherings, and the yearly crop of weddings were all celebrated in manor halls, around market squares, and on village greens. In Kerry and Edinburgh and around Yorkshire and Rhondda lived tribes of dancing people. In those places grew the thriving folk cultures that later came "over the water" to New England.

---

5. Perhaps best envisioned from Breughel's paintings of peasant dances from the 1500s.

The death of Queen Elizabeth in 1603 ushered a number of disturbing forces into British life; eventually civil war strewed English fields with clumps of "Royalist" and "Puritan" dead. The Calvinist influences in the latter group led them to object strenuously to all forms of celebration and to any rituals that strayed outside of the literal written word of the Bible, or that even vaguely reminded of Rome. The Puritans constituted a small and a beleaguered minority at first, and it was out of a desire to worship freely that a number of them began to contemplate emigration to North America. Among these was a group of Separatists later known as the Pilgrims who ventured across the ocean to the frigid shores of Plymouth, Massachusetts, in 1620.

In addition to the Pilgrims of Plymouth and the rough fishermen of Maine and New Hampshire, a host of other English emigrants braved the heaving western sea. Thomas Morton came over in 1622 to a clearing near Quincy, Massachusetts, that was named "Merry Mount." There he helped build a community that hearkened to the old English culture of May Poles, dances, and celebrations. He traded successfully and, by many accounts, caroused heartily with Native peoples at his settlement. Across an island studded harbor came early pioneer Reverend William Blaxton, an Anglican minister who in 1625 became the first European settler to drive a shovel into the soil of the Boston peninsula. He built a house near present-day Charles Street, planted a garden, raised farm animals, and neighbored freely with local Native Americans. In 1630, a number of Puritans who had settled on the arid hills of Charlestown began coming over to Blaxton's homestead to fetch fresh water from his well. As a matter of convenience, they decided to move themselves lock, stock, and testaments over onto the Boston peninsula. Subsequently, between 1630 and 1640, about two thousand people a year began arriving on the coast of Massachusetts Bay.

Once they came to power, the former Puritan minorities began to pillory people who did not share their beliefs. Free-thinkers like Roger Williams, Ann Hutchinson, and William Wainwright were ostracized, punished, and exiled. Quakers William Marmaduke,

Mary Dyer, William Robinson, and William Leddra were hanged on the Boston Common for their beliefs.[6] Thomas Morton was singled out for the attention of the church/state. His relations with the Natives were forbidden, his celebrations and dances condemned, his Maypole was cut down, and he was eventually imprisoned and exiled.[7] The good Reverend Blaxton decided it was time to quit the three hills of Boston, and in 1635 he packed up his library and his other belongings and followed the winds of tolerance and free-thinking off to the site that later became Cumberland, Rhode Island. There he lived out his days in friendship with the Natives. Left to their own devices, the Puritans turned their attention to the business of persecuting witches and to warring with the Pequot, the Wampanoag, and the Wabanaki.

In 1684, the Puritan cleric Increase Mather published a religious treatise that he titled *An Arrow Against Profane and Promiscuous Dancing Drawn Out of the Quiver of the Scriptures*. In it, he declared that "A Dance is the Devils Procession. He that enters into a Dance, enters into his Possession. The Devil is the Guide, the middle and the end of the Dance."[8] After the Salem witch hysteria of 1692–3 subsided, Reverend Cotton Mather added his voice in condemnation of the old English dance traditions, lumping them in with the celebration of Christmas and other holidays as frivolous pastimes

---

6. Many others were subjected to torture by whipping or to exile either back to England or to Rhode Island or New Hampshire.

7. In addition to competing in trade with the Pilgrims, Morton was an Anglican lawyer who represented Sir Ferdinando Gorges in his legal claim to much of what became Massachusetts Bay. Morton wrote *The New English Canaan*, the first book to be banned by the Puritans.

8. "Who were the Inventors of Petulant Dancings? They had not their original amongst the People of God, but amongst the Heathen. Learned men have well observed, that the Devil was the first inventor of the impleaded Dances, and the Gentiles, who worshiped him, the first Practitioners in this Art. They did honour the Devils, whom they served in this way; their Festivals being for the most part spent in Play and Dances." Increase Mather, *An Arrow Against Profane and Promiscuous Dancing Drawn Out of the Quiver of the Scriptures* (Boston: Samuel Green, 1684).

that were deployed as barbed tools in the hands of a wily Satan. Much clerical ink was spilled and hot air was generated regarding dance contact between the sexes. Out of the mouths and agendas of mortals, pronouncements were made about what was and what was not appropriate in the eyes of God.[9]

But by the early 1700s young ministers in the Bay were openly encouraging the use of music in worship. The "singing school" movement spread rapidly, and its proponents like William Billings of Boston and Supply Belcher of Maine began composing "fuguing tunes" that are among the most beautiful musical pieces ever written in America. As a distinct Yankee culture developed on the landscape, the Puritan influence began to recede. In the summer of 1716, while fishing for yellow perch in Spy Pond in what is now Arlington, Massachusetts, Reverend Cotton Mather fell out of his boat and had to make his way safely out from his involuntary immersion in the water.[10] Fishing, we can assume, might have been added to Mather's lengthy list of ill-advised pursuits.

---

9.   Over time, the case has been made for a more lenient look at the Puritans and a reconsideration of their role in setting the course of American history. Certainly there were those among them who were less extreme than others. Judge Samuel Sewall came to openly embrace tolerance and responsibility. Everyone is entitled to their opinion, but in this writer's eyes, taken on the whole, the Puritans are best examined in light of the benchmark "by their fruits ye shall know them." As regards their impact on the life of an American culture that still struggles to be democratic, to be respectful of others, or even just to be libertarian, their inheritance has often asserted itself in the form of complex and bitter fruits.

10. Judge Samuel Sewall in his diary for August 15, 1716 "…Now about Dr. C. Mather Fishing in Spy-pond, falls into the Water, the boat being ticklish, but receives no hurt."

☰ 2 ☰

Fine Fun for Frolicsome Fellows

THE FLOW OF MUSIC AND DANCES among the common people seems to have been unimpeded by the major wars, minor conflicts, and frequent rebellions that flared for years between and among English, Irish, Scottish, French, Spanish, and Dutch political factions. Amidst the constant conflict, many a poor young man felt that his best prospect was to enlist as a soldier or a mercenary in one of the contending forces, and many a young girl lamented that she "had to sell my spinning wheel to buy my love a coat of steel" in the hope that he might survive the wars and come back to her arms in one piece.[11] Throughout the 1700s, immigrants from "the British Isles" came across the Atlantic from hundreds of small towns and villages, many carrying with them little more than their traditions and their hopes for a livable future. The tunes, dance steps, and culture to be found in rural places like Chipping Campden, Stornaway, Bethel Gwynedd, or Balindereen were the

---

11. From Bonnie Dobson's beautiful singing of the Irish song "Shule Aroon." "Sad I sit on Buttermilk Hill/ cry my heart out, cry my fill/ and every tear would turn a mill…"

unique products of generations of local lives and folkways.[12] Rural tunes and dances began making the transatlantic trip in the 1600s and have survived for nearly four hundred years since they came to these shores in the simple yet persistent form of memory swaddled in affection.

These were a disparate set of traditions, largely the product of local heritage that was cross-pollinated over time by various forms of inter-village sharing and the comings and goings of people across the countryside and sometimes over the sea. The tunes were at the heart of the matter, rollicking or pensive, stately or rantipole, romantic, simple, or filigreed as the case might be. Some were so ancient that they had outlived any trace of their source or provenance. Others might have been the work of a country composer, likely a fiddler, whose name and character might be remembered for a time; some had been written on the fife or adapted from the pipes, and many were the work of local or traveling musicians. The tunes were most often constructed in two parts, related but distinct from one another ("A" and "B" sections) that were repeated till all the dancers in the form had gone through their paces, or for as long as anyone had a mind to continue playing. Musicians might appear solo or in a group; in many cases a lone fiddle was considered sufficient, perhaps with a fife or pipes alongside. Over time, drums, lutes, "gitterns," additional strings or wind instruments, and eventually the pianoforte all made appearances as well.

Next ingredient was the dancers themselves in whatever number and character convened at a given time and place. In olden days, most would have grown up learning the local steps or at least being acquainted with the popular musical idioms. In a tavern, there might have been just one couple in the act of flirting and dancing in public in time to a single musician; out on a lawn there might have been a

---

12. Random examples, these, out on the countryside between Normandy and Iceland. Our understanding of the richness of local culture expands exponentially when we take Ireland, Scotland, and Wales into equal consideration with England.

half-dozen couples twirling around, or perhaps across a village green a hundred souls swirling in time like a school of mackerel in the bay. Each couple would know the traditional steps, but each would also very likely have developed their personal or coupled "moves": an extra half-step, a jump, a twist of the head or a thrust of arms or hips that was a bit of a physical signature. Some were raucous and some were sedate, but all were enthusiastic. People were well aware of the wisdom of riding a good time for as long as it might last; life was short, war and pestilence were frequent, and joy was where you found it and persisted in keeping it rolling and reeling along.

Then came the dancing master, who chose the course, set the pace, and herded the flock of dancers through its paces like a sheepdog at a fair. Much depended upon this good soul and the knowledge, skills, and mood that was brought to the role. Even-temper, firmness, patience, and adaptability were all key components of the craft. If the musicians were disagreeable, if the dancers were disorganized, or if a drunk or two threatened to careen like a loose cannon on the deck of a ship at sea, it was the master's job to set things right, decisively and with good humor if possible. A dancing master in the olden times was often an itinerant who traveled a circuit and whose reputation could draw scores of people out to a dance, most of whom had just finished a hard day's work and yet were ready to dive into a long night of celebration on the dance floor.

Cultural remembrances and practices were carried from person-to-person through the generations. Scholars and musicians began to write these sorts of things down in publications like John Playford's *The English Dancing Master*[13] printed in London in 1651, which went into eight editions in less than forty years and almost certainly began circulating in America during the colonial period. A collection of old Scottish tunes was gathered by Nathaniel Gow and published in Edinburgh in the 1790s. Succeeding editions of these volumes and others eventually made their way to New England, and where bound books didn't travel, rural callers and fiddlers passed the old

---

13. John Playford, *The English Dancing Master* (London: Harper, 1651).

traditions from person to person. By the 1780s, small, handwritten notebooks of dance steps were being compiled by Yankee dancers like Clement Weeks of Greenland, New Hampshire, and Alexander Dickson of York, Maine, in tune books full of jigs, hornpipes, reels, minuets, and strathspeys.[14] There were many, many other scribes and instructors like them, probably at least one in nearly every town. Eventually some of these began to set up shop in the cities and to advertise their services to parents who wished to have their children learn the grace and good manners that came to be associated with mastery of the dance.

It was during these latter years of the 1700s that the "country dance" began to marinate in the hybrid vigor of Irish, Scottish, and French traditions that cross-pollinated throughout early America. The population was burgeoning, the New England economy, particularly the maritime economy, was thriving, and the hinterlands were quickly being settled. Public buildings and taverns were erected that were large enough to hold dances in, and that, in many cases, had specific features built in like "sprung floors" and "fiddler's thrones"[15] designed and constructed "just-a-purpose" for use in dances. Immigration acted as an accelerant in the development of the dance tradition. Religious persecution brought Peter Faneuil and hundreds of other French Huguenots to Boston in the early 1700s, many from the west-central countryside of France, among

---

14. Joy Van Cleef and Kate Van Winkle Keller, "Selected American Country Dances and Their English Sources" in *Music In Colonial Massachusetts, Volume 1* (Boston: Colonial Society of Massachusetts, 1980). The Old York Historical Society in York, Maine, has Alexander Dickson's tune book in its collections, along with the handmade fiddle of lighthouse keeper Eliphalet Grover.

15. Carpenters became adept at constructing dance floors, usually on an upper level of a building, that rested on "floating floor joists" that flexed along with the rhythm of the dancers. Elevated seats or "thrones" were built that allowed the fiddler to sit at a level above the floor in order that his notes could carry over the tread of the dancers.

them craftsmen like Appolos Rivoire.[16] Scotch-Irish came over the water from Ulster; they settled Londonderry, New Hampshire in 1719 and soon thereafter reportedly planted the first hill of potatoes in America. All these settlers brought the traditions of home, hearth, and village dance floor along with them.

The prospects for the success of the American Revolution depended greatly upon the ability of the patriot forces to attract the support of France to their cause. Benjamin Franklin was dispatched to Paris in 1776 and remained there representing American interests for nearly a decade. By the spring of 1777, sympathetic French sources were shipping over thousands of Charleville muskets which were unloaded at the Portsmouth, New Hampshire, docks and quickly distributed to the Yankee hinterlands in support of the rebel cause. After patriot victories at Bennington and Saratoga the following summer and fall, Franklin persuaded France to openly join forces with American farmers and ultimately tipped the scale of the Revolution towards victory. Regiments of French soldiers in pastel and cream-colored uniforms and fleets of sailors from the trim frigates of the French Navy made landfall in Boston and Newport during the course of four remaining years of the war. In that refined day, diplomacy, military strategy, and finance were matters to be taken up at the ballroom and banquet table as much as they were to be discussed within the confines of a conference room. The Americans rejoiced in having a skilled and enthusiastic dancer as their commander-in-chief; references abound regarding George Washington's triumphs on the dance floor, and, in particular, to his affection for the piece called "Sir Roger de Coverley."[17]

---

16. Rivoire's son apprenticed as a silver smith in Boston under the Anglicized name of Paul Revere.

17. Ralph Page notes that heavy French influence was "due to the influence of early dancing masters....many of them sailed over with the French troops during the Revolution, and, seeing the possibilities of following their professions on these shores, they never sailed back." Ralph Page and Beth Tolman, *The Country Dance Book* (New York: Barnes & Co., 1937), 60.

Styles and customs came over from all corners of the Old World, and by the 1780s the contradance repertoire was firmly established as the favorite in New England. The blending of English and French country dance styles quickened the pace in American parlors and dance halls. In 1787, John Quincy Adams wrote that "at about seven o'clock we met at the dancing hall, and from that time till between three and four in the morning we were continually dancing."[18] The popularity of the contradance is reflected in printed collections of dance steps that were decorated with engravings of ladies in gowns and gentlemen in wigs and high-heeled shoes, all gathering expectantly in facing lines. One can easily imagine a tune like "Sweet Richard" working its stately and fanciful way through the glowing halls of John Hancock's mansion high above the Boston Common, chairs shifting and gowns swishing as eager couples took to the gleaming floors. Doubtless some thoughtful person would reach over and give the fiddler a dram.

In the village era, barn-raisings, corn-huskings, and other community work became occasions when people "danced all night till broad daylight." Weddings were socially consummated at country dances in a time when "most towns of any consequence usually had access to some rustic fiddler who turned out to be the life of the party." Every town or region had a noteworthy fiddle player who would perform for a few coppers; a number of these were African slaves. Cuffee Whipple of Portsmouth held court at "maizy dances" in the Assembly House in the old seaport town,[19] and in Canterbury, New Hampshire, a Black man named Sampson Battis "was a famous fiddler and for many years afforded fine fun for frolicsome fellows in

---

18. Cited in Michael McKernan's delightful "Brattleboro Dawn Dances History," *The Wayback Machine.* https://web.archive.org/web/20011211125057/http://www.dawndance.org:80/history.html.

19. Located at the corner of Vaughn St. and Rait's Court in Portsmouth, the Assembly House was built in 1750, was divided into halves in 1838, and, incredibly, was demolished in 1970s. George Washington attended a ball here in November of 1789, and says in his diary that it was one of the finest dances he had ever been to.

Concord." Following their service in the Revolution, both these men were granted their freedom.[20]

Unlikely as it had seemed, the Americans prevailed over the British, peace was eventually established, and, after a period of domestic unrest, the Constitution was duly ratified. From about 1790 until the Industrial Revolution of the 1830s, America enjoyed a sort of a golden age in a time that used to be described in history books as an "era of good feelings." New England reaped from the world economy through its fisheries, its lumber ports, its shipyards, and its distilleries. The War of 1812 ratified the young nation's independence, and the victory of the USS *Constitution* over the HMS *Guerriere* presented Yankee musicians with the inspiration to write "Hull's Victory," a dance tune that has remained popular for generations. New Hampshire native Daniel Webster was among America's most potent political forces, combining his influence with men like President John Quincy Adams of Massachusetts, Commander Edward Preble of Maine, and the financial capacities of the Perkins, Russell, and Heard families whose empires stretched from State Street around the treacherous straits of the Horn to San Francisco. From there it was a long jaunt across the Pacific through uncharted coral reefs, fleets of Malay pirates, and random typhoons to the docks and counting houses of Canton, Foochow, and Shanghai.[21]

Newton F. Tolman devoted years to the study of Anglo-American tunes, particularly pieces performed from about 1750 to 1850, a period he referred to as a "golden age" of traditional dance music. In an interview in 1972, he described the dynamic involved in the refinement of the old country dance tunes: "Some of the best musicians were playing the music, employed by some of the richest

---

20. Louis Pichierri, *Music In New Hampshire 1623–1800* (New York: Columbia University Press, 1960), 25 and 55.

21. In 1794, the Boston-built ship *Empress of China* arrived in Canton carrying silver and thirty tons of ginseng, and sailed back home loaded with tea and silk. In short order, otter skins from the Oregon coast became the trade medium that supported the fabled China Trade.

and most discriminating patrons of the social world. It was also during that period when most musical instruments were redesigned and perfected much as we know them today, and afforded greatly improved techniques in play."[22] The result was the vigorous mix of rural folk roots and musical sophistication that Tolman devoted much of his life to reviving.

Dances, balls, and impromptu shindigs were the major social forces in a nation full of new accomplishment, unbounded optimism, and good humor. Diaries from the period reveal the potent place that social dance played in the life of young America. The sighting of a fiddle in the snow-covered saddlebags of a traveler taking a room at a remote inn might draw a crowd of local people who urged him to take a seat in the tavern so he could lead the village in a contradance. In Portsmouth on Thanksgiving afternoon in 1805, a dance commenced that kept its young participants on the floor until half past one in the morning. In scrapbooks and family papers, engraved notices can still be found announcing dances held in places like Orange, Vermont, Peterborough, New Hampshire, and Worcester, Massachusetts, listing time, place, the "committee of arrangements," the "floor managers," and the musical accompaniment of groups like "Goddard and Twitchell's Quadrille Band."

By the 1820s, an Annual Stageman's Ball was being held at the Grecian Hall of the Eagle Coffee House in Concord, New Hampshire, drawing men and women from throughout New England at the invitation of a committee of arrangements comprised of over sixty stagecoach drivers from three states. "Most of the drivers wore long pants, fitting close to their shoes, tail coats and blue, red, or yellow vests, while the women and girls had flowers and ribbons and bows of velvet in their hair, and dresses with skirts so big that in dancing they bellowed out on the floor. Supper was sumptuous...for dancing the hall had a sprung floor, and you could soon feel it rise and fall

---

22. Newton Tolman quoted in "New Hampshire Author Tells of his Long Search for Authentic Square Dance Music" by WBR in *The Milford, N.H. Cabinet and Wilton Journal*, December 14, 1972.

under the weight of a hundred and sixty couples of husky drivers and their daughters, sweethearts, and wives dancing polkas, waltzes, jigs, and reels!"[23]

The love of dance pulsed across time, gender, race, age, and social position. In his travels through the wilderness of upstate New York in the 1790s, Francois Chateaubriand is said to have encountered a clearing in the woods filled with "a score of painted savages dancing quadrilles to a violin. It was played by a frizzled little Frenchman, with powdered locks and muslin ruffles, whom the Indians had retained as a dancing-master in exchange for the hams of bears and beaver skins."[24] In 1823, the bicentennial of the settlement of New Hampshire was observed at ceremonies held in Portsmouth, including a dance at a "filled to overflowing hall" presided over by Daniel and Grace Webster. "Grandsire and grandams danced in the same sets with their children and grandchildren."[25] All was "gain and good prospects," in a generation when New Hampshire's abolitionist Hutchinson Family Singers would soon proclaim that the national motto was "Go Ahead!"[26]

Contradance tunes, fuguing hymns, and broadside ballads were the bedrock musical forms of the most vigorous era in our history, partly because they required, in fact, they were defined by, *personal participation*. In the tavern or on a street corner, a ballad singer could count on being joined in at least on the chorus by a raft of raucous voices and stamping feet. On Sundays, in stately meeting houses, congregations were expected to sing along on

---

23. From a letter archived in the collections of the N.H. Historical Society, reproduced in *Taverns and Stagecoaches of New England* by Allan Forbes, Boston: State Street Bank and Trust, 1953, 89.

24. Van Wyck Brooks, *The World of Washington Irving* (New York: E.F. Dutton, 1944), 41.

25. Richard M. Candee "New Hampshire's Centennial Celebration" in *New England Celebrates,* (Boston: Dublin Folklife Series, Boston University, 2000), 59.

26. "Uncle Sam's Farm," written in 1848 by Jesse Hutchinson, and sung by the Hutchinson Family Singers of Milford, New Hampshire.

fuguing tunes with choirs who had spent all Saturday evening practicing their soaring four-part harmonies. And on the dance floor, the stroke of a fiddle would bring people up and out of their seats, expectantly coupling-up in line before the name of a dance was announced.

America has seldom taken the opportunity to quit while it was ahead, and neither politics, economics, or culture has ever gathered much moss or accumulated much perspective in the course of our events. The Industrial Revolution brought swift and profound changes to American attitudes and habits. Modernity began to shift people away from the active position of being *producers* and towards the role of being *consumers*. This passivity may have begun in music when it became more fashionable to become part of an *audience* instead of being a *participant*. Culture split into roughly two levels of stratification: the *refined* and the *popular*. Members of the artistic elite in Boston, New York, and Charleston began taking their cues from the concert halls and the salons of Europe. The rise of chamber music led to the importation of scores of classical musicians and a proliferation of string quartets and symphony orchestras in Boston and elsewhere. Instrumentalists became thought of as being *performers* more readily than they were considered to be *artists*. The old tunes fell out of sophisticated favor.

Around the same time, at street level, a bizarre incarnation of America's burdensome racial dynamics was promoted in the "minstrel shows," which swapped bigotry, vulgarity, and snappy tunes for ready cash. None of this could be considered "art," except in the case of the more gifted compositions of Stephen Foster, whose alcohol-fueled expressions of sentiment, longing, and displacement became the first national popular music "hits." After gold was discovered near Sacramento in 1849, many a young man felt ready to set out for California with a banjo on his knee.

The profound rupture of the Civil War jolted America away from the integrity and the vigor of its foundations. Broadside ballads went extinct. The beautiful old fuguing tunes disappeared completely. Few were published after 1830 and none seem to have been recorded until as late as 1965.[27] Contradance traditions retreated up into the seams and nooks of the uplands like a troop of Jacobite rebels, tunes and steps kept alive in hill and hinterland until such time as the bonnie old music might "come back again." In the years between the Civil War and the Roaring Twenties, populations plummeted in the small towns of the North Country. Villages that were never invaded by the railroad or the turnpike remained culturally rooted in the stage-coach era.

Depopulation brought abject poverty into many rural areas when the longstanding barter traditions of local economies were displaced or dismantled. "Cash was king" in the modern world. The image of a remote farm in the back-country was ready fodder for urban caricature, peopled by a booted, bearded, bewildered hick peering out from his sagging porch and his corncob-smoking wife stirring a fry-pan full of salt pork in her kitchen while drinking from the tepid nose of her teakettle. Many of the poor abandoned stricken farms and took marginal jobs as "wage slaves" in or near the mill-towns, and thousands of rickety homesteads fell to rack and ruin by the 1880s. Still, there remained up in the hills a hardy collection of canny and capable Yankee farm families, augmented by resourceful settlers from French Canada and central Europe and well-to-do city rusticators, none of whom felt the need to imagine living anywhere else.

They all held assets that they preferred to manage without ostentation. They protected their privacy as much as they valued their independence. Jointly and severally, they took pains to keep a decent roof on the old post-and-beam culture of farms, lyceums, recitals, dances, and fairs. In places like Nelson and Tamworth, Deerfield, Belfast, and Tunbridge, the ancient contradance tunes mellowed in stout barrels of rural idiosyncrasy, much as they had known in the places that they had been birthed in, centuries before, over on the far

---

27. The rich inheritance of Billings and others was reclaimed in a Folkways recording made at Old Sturbridge Village; Old Sturbridge Singers, *New England Harmony*, Folkways FA 2377.

side of the Atlantic. Up in the countryside, the old ways persevered while American popular culture fattened on the greed of the Gilded Age and as the teeming cities hustled themselves off towards the conundrums of the twentieth century.[28]

---

28. As hopeful and inspiring as the hymn "America" was when it was written by Wellesley College's Katharine Lee Bates in 1893, the nation's "alabaster cities" were not long "undimmed by human tears."

The Hub of Twentieth-Century New England

AMERICA ENTERED INTO A MODERN ERA that would largely be defined by the progress and expansion of its cities. Railroads and highways jackhammered their ways across the continent, conquering what remained of the wilderness and the western frontier. In the settled areas of New England, cities filled with immigrants and nearby towns were subdivided and developed into "suburbs." Indoor plumbing was introduced during the 1880s, and within a few generations its use was universal in metropolitan areas. Office workers took the train into their jobs in Boston, returning home to the anthills of commuter towns that grew around the city core. Depending upon class and education, "the heads of households" were employed either as office workers, wearing suits and loud ties and securing their trousers with belts, or as open-throated laborers who wore coveralls or work clothes held up with suspenders. Most middle-class women were full-time "housewives" or "homemakers," although a growing number were being trained on the campus of Katherine Gibbs College for secretarial positions and later for executive careers in a number of fields.

By the 1920s, gas ranges were the chief cooking medium in homes. Some families owned electric refrigerators but many still kept their food in insulated oaken "iceboxes" and had blocks of ice delivered weekly by "icemen" who plodded the streets in horse-drawn wagons. Oil heat was gaining in popularity, but many people still warmed their homes from coal furnaces in their basements. Anthracite was mined in Kentucky and came up to New England on trains and ships, then was heaved through cellar windows and down basement bulkheads. There it was piled close enough to be shoveled into a glowing furnace that forced hot water up into crackling radiators that were located in every room. Coal smoke issued forth out of chimneys in homes and factories and up into the great forgiving greenhouse in the sky, where it had already been accumulating for a century. In Boston and its suburbs, everybody had electricity and most people had running water and flush toilets. An hour away from Beacon Hill, you might enter realms where wood heat, kerosene lamps, and outhouses still could be found. In the city, men smoked Camels, Chesterfields, and Lucky Strikes; out in the country, members of both sexes might still be encountered who took their tobacco in the form of snuff.

Most of Boston's beef was coming in from the west, but annually about thirty thousand live head of cattle and one hundred thousand sheep were still being "dressed off" in a forty-acre slaughterhouse complex located in Brighton that, until the 1950s, drained directly into the Charles River. Fish were gutted and dressed by practiced hands on ships from Boston, Gloucester, and New Bedford, where wooden schooners named after saints and sweethearts docked daily with catches netted or hooked out in the fertile Gulf of Maine or on the Grand Banks of Newfoundland. Vegetables and fruit were raised on farms as close as Lexington, Walpole, and Arlington, delivered either to locally owned grocery stores or in Boston to streets carpeted with fragments of cabbage, strawberries, and lettuce in front of the teeming stalls of Faneuil Hall and Haymarket Square. In most cases, family-owned neighborhood stores were the source of groceries, most of them fresh, although there were a few regional companies marketing canned products like Burnham and Morrill's Baked Beans and Snow's Clam Chowder. Hood's and Whiting's dairies provided customers with the home delivery of milk, and most neighborhoods still had a local bakery.[29]

Vigorous cultural expression merged with mercantile interests at Christmas time, when stores in downtown Boston displayed a stunning array of toys, leading with the incredible model train sets that ran non-stop at Jordan Marsh. Every store window was a wonderland, and the city streets teemed with vigorous small businesses like Ehrlich's Tobacconists, Goodspeed's Bookstore, and S.S. Pierce's, whose founder declared in 1831 that "I may not make money, but I shall make a reputation" and then proceeded to do both quite handily. Sundaes and chocolate sodas could be found at Bailey's and at Brigham's. Durgin-Park, the Union Oyster House, Warmouth's Port Side, Loch Ober, and Jacob Wirth's were among the many iconic restaurants in an old town where a good tipper might be remembered for decades by Irish or Italian waitresses.

"Elevated trains" ran on railways built high up on iron scaffolds throughout Boston in the 1880s to avoid street collisions with horse-powered wagons. The last horse-drawn trolley in Boston was converted to electric power on Marlborough Street around 1900, but the garages that housed street-cars and busses in Cambridge and Jamaica Plain were referred to as "car barns" for years. Trains, trolley cars, and busses were the chief forms of transportation. Commercial air travel was in its infancy; the Boston and Maine Railroad held controlling interest in the only regional airline. In thick weather, the pilots had to fly low enough to sight-navigate by following the courses of shoreline, roads and railroad tracks. By 1930, many families owned an automobile, and paved two-lane roads connected cities and towns throughout New England. Some automobile mechanics operated out of buildings that had previously been occupied by blacksmith shops. Almost no one pumped their own gasoline. Uniformed, capped attendants came out, took an order to "fill 'er up!" or for a specific amount, washed the windshield, offered to check the oil,

---

29. Both major Boston dairy companies originated in New Hampshire: H.P. Hood in Derry and Whiting in Wilton.

took cash from the driver and made change if necessary. And off you went, into the twentieth century, without a seatbelt.

Republicans read the *Boston Herald-Traveler* or the *Boston Post,* educated liberals read the *Boston Globe,* and blue-collar people read the tabloid *Record-American,* which still fondly recalled the late war with Spain. Morning and evening editions were printed of all newspapers in order to keep readers up-to-date on the investments they made in the stock market or at the race track. In most years, the Bruins competed for hockey's Stanley Cup with the Black Hawks, and the Red Wings. The Red Sox finished last for nearly an entire decade. Neither the Celtics nor the Patriots were in existence. There were no professional African-American athletes in New England.[30]

Class, gender, race, ethnicity, religion, and education were cards that were dealt out at birth, to be played as best as could be through life. It *was* possible, in America, to make an end-run around some of the ethnic boundaries, if you were gifted, athletic, beautiful, or shrewd enough to do so. But the socio-economic territory enforced between the entitled upper class and the insecure middle class was the dynamic that ruled America's cultural roost as rigidly as the order to be found in the dust and cobwebs of any chicken house. In the triple-deckers, the working class rolled up its sleeves, dried its hands on faded aprons, and dealt with practical matters.

New England was, far and away, the section of the country with the longest recorded history, and one possessed with one of the stronger senses of American regionality. But by the twentieth century, mass media in the form of radio and movies had begun to assert a commercial version of modern cultural infallibility. City and suburb fell into the temptation to treat their traditions like a series of quaint "ye olde" episodes rather than as a dynamic inheritance, more like a drowsy, addled geezer than a vigorous and engaging elder.

---

30.   Don Newcombe and Roy Campanella broke organized baseball's color line with the Nashua Dodgers in 1946; the Boston Celtics brought in Bill Russell in 1956, and Pumpsie Green joined the Boston Red Sox, the last Major League Baseball team to integrate, in 1959.

By the 1930s, New England had descended into hard times, as the ragtime era, the can-do spirit that followed World War I, and the razz-a-ma-tazz of the "Roaring 20s" ran themselves straight into the brick wall of the Great Depression. More than a quarter of the men in Massachusetts suddenly found themselves unemployed. Banks and businesses failed, and thousands of families that had always considered themselves to be financially secure saw their social status evaporate along with their savings. Even some of the Brahmins were seen in frayed collars, and the phrase "keeping up appearances" crept into the lexicon. People took refuge from harsh economics in the addictive fantasy-world of radio and movie entertainment, and the concocted "reality" of mass media began to establish a firm beachhead in the modern American mind. There was welcome distraction to be found in the affairs of the cinematic royalty who cavorted under the carefree fronds of Palm Beach and Palm Springs. Modern America's attitude towards the old New England culture might best be summed up in the title of one of the biggest popular song hits of the 1930s: "Thanks for the Memory."

≡ 4 ≡

Arlington Aggie

AROUND BOSTON and the crowded mouth of the Charles, the urban peninsula was ringed with suburbs, the landscape kept attractive and, in places, natural by virtue of a series of parks, reservations, and small ponds. The busy route from Cambridge to Lexington where Paul Revere once rode a borrowed horse had come to be called Massachusetts Avenue, crossing Alewife Brook at the traffic lights on the border between the city of Cambridge and the growing town of Arlington. Amidst the honking of Chevrolets on Route 2 and under the sigh of the northwest wind in elm branches, Dudley Laufman's story begins.

He was born on February 7, 1931, the eldest child of Miller and Marjorie Laufman. His family lived on the corner of Pleasant Street and Gould Road on a south-facing hillside overlooking Spy Pond in Arlington, Massachusetts. The Laufmans became Quakers, holding to a faith and a corresponding world view that were quite distinct from the prevailing Congregational and Catholic cultures of Massachusetts. Dudley had two sisters, Ann and Janet, and two brothers, Alan and Philip. He was something of an indifferent student who remembers that he had "no inclination to be a clerk," an occupation that could be seen as the baseline common expectation of that time and place. "Arlington was my home town," he recalls, "I was one of the gang. Played baseball and hockey." A highlight of his

25

early life was the New England Hurricane of September 21, 1938; a low point occurred when he was placed by school officials in a "slow" class in junior high. Dudley's mom and dad were supportive parents of a son who, from the start of boyhood, rambled along to his own tune. He was later to say that by the age of six he knew that his future lay, somewhere and somehow, out in the countryside.

The Laufman family spent their summers at a vacation home on Long Island, New Hampshire, out in the middle of Lake Winnipesaukee. There they were visited by a couple named Chandler, fellow Boston University alums who summered in Raymond, New Hampshire. In 1945, when it became clear that young Dudley was failing to thrive in the Arlington school system, the thought occurred that the boy might gain from visiting the farm where the Chandlers got their dairy products. One thing led to another, and that June, after his sophomore year ended, young Dudley made his way to Fremont and a summer job at Mistwold Farm, which was owned and operated by the Quimby family. The Mistwold herd of Jersey cows was the heart and soul of the dairy; Dudley visited and immediately took to the cows and the way of life on the farm, where he worked again during the following two summers. On his birthday in 1948, his mother drove him in a snowstorm to visit the Norfolk County Agricultural School in Walpole, Massachusetts. There he was informed that "the barn was the classroom," a concept that struck him as a vast improvement on his educational experiences in the starchy public schools of Arlington.

In the late 1940s, Dudley's father decided that vacation property on "the big lake" was too pricey, and so he cast his eye elsewhere in search of a rural summer cottage. By the time Dudley was in high school, his dad had settled on the idea of a place over in the Monadnock region, tucked into the little hill town of Nelson, New Hampshire. This was a fateful choice, since the Laufmans were thus venturing into an isolated Yankee village where the founding culture remained intact and vital. Neither railroad nor turnpike had come through town in the nineteenth century. What remained unalloyed was a cadre of people, natives and newcomers, who believed in combining personality, tradition, music, and community in the interest of having a good time. Events were still routine in Nelson that were unheard of in nearby Hillsborough, let alone in Boston or New York.

Dudley attended classes in Walpole, Massachusetts, at the Norfolk Agricultural School in 1948, 1949, and 1950. The school was set on a 365-acre campus[31] and featured a forty-by-one-hundred-foot dairy barn that had been built two years after the 1917 founding of "the Aggie." Dudley's experience at Mistwold Farm stood him in good stead as he mastered a curriculum that covered all aspects of farm practice and management. The regional agricultural economy was specializing in Holstein and Guernsey cattle, Barred Plymouth Rock and New Hampshire Red hens, and McIntosh apples. Dudley became acquainted with pomologist Elmore Ashman, who taught fruit culture and organized square dances with his wife, piano player Maude Ashman. Dances were held at the school, and young Dudley was captivated, finding himself channeling the shades of all sorts of ancient traditions. In his Arlington home, he set up a miniature model farm on the ping-pong table in his basement, with a barn complete with cattle stanchions made of clothespins.

In their new summer place in the Monadnock region, the Laufmans became acquainted with the Helwigs, a Quaker family from Larchmont, New York, who had two daughters and who also summered at a place in Nelson. They got to know a genial local man named Frank Upton, and through him and others, they began to absorb the creative native character of the community they had moved into. While he was still in high school, Dudley went with his mother to the dance at the old Nelson Town Hall, where Shorty Durant did the calling for a band that hailed from Winchendon, Massachusetts. Dudley danced his first contradance with his mom

---

31. Norfolk County Agricultural High School is still a thriving institution, with six hundred students enrolled in programs including Agricultural Mechanics, Animal Science, Environmental Science, and Horticultural Science on the Main Street, Walpole campus.

to the swing of "Hull's Victory," a tune that had been written in celebration of the USS *Constitution's* defeat of the HMS *Guerriere* off Nova Scotia on August 19, 1812. The Helwigs decided to hold a dinner party in Nelson to introduce the Laufmans to the local folks, including the many members of the Tolman clan, who had lived in Nelson since before the Revolution. During the social exchanges of the event, young Dudley fell into a conversation with classically trained flautist Newton Tolman (1908–1986). At some point, the young man found reason to fish a harmonica out of his jacket pocket and launched into the ancient contra tune "Durang's Hornpipe." The middle-aged Tolman was appropriately amazed, and an improbable and deep relationship was cemented on the spot.

Dudley began calling dances in 1947; reportedly, "The Crooked Stovepipe" was his first dance. He was declaring himself the master of his own fate on the shores of Spy Pond as emphatically as Admiral Farragut ever did on Mobile Bay, making the jump from being a square peg in a round hole into being a young man on a self-defined mission: accordion at the ready, and pegs, holes, and torpedoes be damned.

≡ 5 ≡

Mistwold Farm and
the Dancing Yankee Countryside

BEFORE POSTWAR SUBURBAN SPRAWL, the paved and settled area around Boston did not spread out much further than what would later become the famed circumference of Route 128, "America's Technology Highway." Towns like Lexington and Walpole were still rural; there were dairies in Stoneham and Concord, chicken farms in Reading, and a vast set of piggeries spread themselves out aromatically just south of Andover. Although nowhere near as self-sufficient as she had been in the nineteenth century, New England was still producing much of her own food, particularly in dairy products, poultry, apples, and cranberries. South of the White Mountains, agriculture still thrived across the fertile New Hampshire countryside.

Fremont, New Hampshire, the site of Mistwold Farm, is located in the coastal plain, not far from Exeter, and only about a half hour inland from the Atlantic Ocean. In 1730, an agent of the British crown had come through the territory to make sure that the local settlers were not stealing "the King's pines," trees big enough to be set aside for use by the Royal Navy. "Citizens disguised as Indians" made him feel less than welcome, chasing him away in what came to be called "The Mast Tree Riot." In addition to its farms, the town became known for a huge brickyard that was said to have produced five million bricks a year and the Spaulding and Frost cooperage that has crafted fifty million quality wooden barrels since it was founded in the 1870s. In 1854, the town was named after abolitionist John C. Frémont, the first Republican candidate for president, who ran on the slogan "Free Soil, Free Men, and Frémont."

In 2009, when *Boston Globe* writer Scott Alarik interviewed Dudley Laufman about his time at Mistwold Farm, he described "an awkward, quiet, painfully shy boy who felt like a stranger everywhere he went."[32] In light of the fact that during the nearly eighty years since he left Fremont, Dudley Laufman has made a living performing before large groups of people, it could be assumed that the experience there was a transformative one. When Alarik asked him if he could sum up the vision of his life's work, he answered, simply, "Well, the vision is Mistwold Farm." In a variation on the town's namesake, we might speculate that the time spent on the farm was an exercise in "Free Soil, Free Men, and Free Dudley Laufman."

In the late 1960s, radical young people would spill out of the cities to try their hands at the "back to the land" movement. In 1945, there was no such generational groundswell. For Dudley, Mistwold Farm was a solo flight into a whole new natural world, one that he would remember in song as "where the cardinal flowers grow, and the mist arises so, and the whip-poor-wills sing in the meadow below."[33] Whether he knew it consciously or not, in the lyrics to his tune "Mistwold," Dudley was focusing on iconic wildlife species that were fast disappearing from a suburbanized New England landscape. Something was calling to the young man, and he ventured off into the wild on the vision quest that would determine his life's course.

In the process of making that personal journey, Dudley had to master the transition from acting on an unthinking and conditioned suburban frame of reference to deciding to see the world through the

---

32. Scott Alarik in the *Boston Globe*, "Preserving the Spirit of the Dance" July 24, 2009.

33. Dudley Laufman in "Mistwold," by the Canterbury Country Dance Orchestra, F&W Records FW 5, 1974.

eyes and from the heart of a farmer. This process was an enormous and a difficult adjustment, since it demanded all the insecurity of immigration, with all the mispronunciations, awkwardness, loneliness, and embarrassments attendant to the risky business of cultural displacement. In Dudley's case, he was motivated by two extraordinarily compelling forces: traditional music and indigenous farming. These were not "countercultures." They were Yankee bedrock, ways of life that were rooted in every watershed, intervale, village, and ridgeline in New England.

Farming resembles country dancing in that it is all about participation. You are either "all in" or, really, you are not in at all. But, unlike a dancer, the small farmer is usually acting pretty much by him- or herself. A farmer internalizes a level of personal responsibility-in-the-moment that most modern folks do not understand. If you don't do something on the farm, it won't get done. If you are given three good sunny days in June when your hay is just at the right maturity, you *have* to cut it and put it in the barn while you have the chance. If you don't plant your corn early enough in June, it will not mature before the first frost kills the plants in September. You cannot tell a cow in labor that her timing is inconvenient and that she'll have to reschedule the arrival of her calf. If you weren't brought up with this sense of responsibility in the world, you have to embrace it consciously and make it a core element of your personality. This was a trait that was well understood by the founding generations, nearly all of whom had been farmers, but in the modern era this sort of outlook was becoming completely unknown.

Anyone who shares a life with dairy cattle commits into a profound connection with husbandry and hard work. Eons ago, milk cows entered into a life compact with human beings, who generally rank among the less dependable creatures on the planet. In regard to the cows in his care, young Dudley made promises of a sort that a good dairyman never outlives. In order to survive in health and security, a cow provides nourishment, trust, and companionship, and she has to be able to receive the same back in trade. Since she also throws her calf and all her manure into the bargain, any farmer with a conscience (or even just the self-interest of the profit-motive) learns to treat the responsibility of cow care more like a vow than a job.

And so Dudley learned about the daily ebb and flow of life with a herd of dairy cows. Milk and shit, feed and water, hay and fences, ovulation, sex, conception, birth and afterbirth, lactation, good health and bad, and decline, death, and decomposition are all on the docket, come rain or shine. Cows thrive on routine and distrust chaos; they have a lot to teach people. The young man became adept at the faithful repetition of chores, played out in all the opportunities and obligations that come with the seasons and the flow of time that never reverses if it is wasted. All this became a combination of undergraduate work and boot camp training, measured in full pails of buttery milk and in the sweet-smelling breath of Jersey cows. Dudley was earning the right to be considered dependable by the sort of rural people that he would be dealing with for the rest of his life.

In the forefront of those persons were Jonathan (Bucky) and Betty Quimby, the owners of the Mistwold dairy farm. Dudley describes the couple as "real old-time New Englanders," hard-working people who had at one point, soldiered through a disastrous barn fire without losing a cow or missing a milking. It was after that fire that they bought the farm in Fremont that Dudley went to, first for a weekend visit, then a summer, and eventually for the sophomore year in 1947 that he attended at Raymond High School. In addition to all the other aspects of farm life, the Quimbys were full participants in the tradition of New England country dances. "Bucky played the fiddle and Betty had that old Henry Ford *Good Morning* book, and they had dances, junkets, in the kitchen."[34]

On many evenings, the day's work was followed by one of those kitchen dance junkets. "I was just getting used to girls, so dancing

---

34. "Henry Ford's *Good Morning* book provided illustrated instructions on the proper steps and deportment for old-fashioned dancing—it was part of Ford's crusade to revive the dances of his youth. Written by Ford's dancing master Benjamin Lovett, much research went into it, based upon old dance manuals and interviews with "old-timers." First printed in 1926, the book sold widely for many years." From the Henry Ford Museum website.

with them was exciting enough. But it was the whole atmosphere, the woodsmoke, the sound of the fiddle, the firelight on the girl's hair. It was a real community dance, and that spirit has stuck with me straight through."[35] With his life revolving between Arlington, Walpole, and, eventually, Amherst, Massachusetts; Fremont, Nelson, and later Canterbury, New Hampshire; and Brattleboro and Plymouth, Vermont; Dudley Laufman could not have constructed an itinerary better calculated to immerse himself in what still remained alive of America's most venerable country dance traditions.

The realm of folk dance has been both provoking definition and confounding it for a thousand years. Dancers of all sorts have been central figures in the raucous, joyful lives of country towns from the days of crofters and castles to those of farmers and freeholders. Individual dances thrived in small villages all over the landscape, spread by itinerant musicians and perhaps livened up when a sailor lad came back to his home town with a salty new set of jigs and hornpipes in his kit bag. The tunes could be easily memorized, but as time went on, everyone had to pay attention when the caller ventured onto the floor and ran through the dance steps. With practice came confidence, then perhaps even a bit of a swagger, since "there is nothing like the realization of your own style to make you feel like the biggest pumpkin in the row."[36]

Earnest eye-witnesses from earlier times left wildly varying accounts of a body of rural dances that took on a staggering variety of shapes and forms. For example, in contemporary accounts of Shaker dances, we can find descriptions that cover a range of motion from stepping in reverential group movements to writhing solo and prone on the floor, both of which might have been accurate. The era between the 1750s and the 1840s was a particularly dynamic time in

---

35. Scott Alarik, op. cit.
36. Ralph Page and Beth Tolman, *The Country Dance Book* (New York: Barnes & Co., 1937), 28.

our young country. Community-building, agriculture, immigration, reform, and invention were all in the process of moving forward in the glow of national optimism. Regional identity was a by-product of hearth and wilderness, of wealth from blue-water voyages, and in the hundreds of lyceums, academies, and meetinghouses where citizens endeavored to find "a better world." People danced a whole lot more in the long ages before modern times than they do now. Rather than going to the movies, surfing the web, or shopping, couples who found time on their hands grabbed hold of each other and danced.

Young America was quick to latch on to a new dance, as in the case of the quadrille, which was remembered as "being hatched in the French court ballet…it so fascinated everybody that it immediately took hold like measles in a kindergarten. It whisked its way across the channel, and after getting well established in the British Isles, it found its way to America."[37] Customs and idioms shifted; there were no import duties charged on music at the borders, translations were not required to play the tunes, and nobody needed either a license or a diploma to run a dance. American country dance flamed brightly for a few generations before falling out of fashion and retreating to the hills when the days of the stagecoach ended and the era of the railroads began to emerge just before the Civil War.

Much as would be the case with ragtime a bit later on, country dances were shared among the social classes and across the boundaries of wealth. Invention came from the coastline and tradition reigned in the hinterlands. Refinement and popularity sprang from the urban well-to-do, who began employing both singing and dancing masters to instruct their children in learning the inspirational fuguing tunes and the mannerly dance steps of the era. A hybrid repertoire developed that incorporated elements of traditional Anglo-Irish jigs, reels, and hornpipes with the more flowing dances of couples in facing lines that was variously referred to as country dances, contradances, and, in France, *contratanzes*. In the Pioneer Valley of Massachusetts, an African-American named John Putnam played left-handed fiddle

---

37. Ibid., p. 58.

and led the popular contradance orchestra that was named after him and that played throughout a wide swath of river and hill towns between the 1850s and the 1890s. Years later, it was remembered that "he had peculiar ability in playing the contra tunes, executing jigs, reels and hornpipes so seductively that the most rheumatic legs were inspired to perform with the greatest agility…Back in the eighties dances usually began at 8 in the evening and did not end until three or four o'clock in the morning, the programs including some 30 or more dances. This put a heavy task on orchestras, which had to play through that number of dances, divided between quadrilles and contradances, with a few waltzes and polkas interspersed, which made a fairly full night."[38]

In the 1920s, New England folklorist Eloise Linscott outlined some definitions of terms: "Contra, circle, and square are the names of different formations included in the general designation, country dance. In different localities, the country dance may be given the name of one of the formations; thus in some areas the term "square dance," "contry dance," or "line dance" indicates that these formations will predominate in the evening's program. The *square dance* is usually a "quadrille," with the couples forming a square; the *quadrille* is a reel of four couples; the "contry" as the Yankee calls it (or "line dance") is rightly termed "contra," and is a dance of opposite lines of couples; the *circle* or "round" dance arranges all the dancers in a huge ring around the hall. The *waltz* and *polka*, developments on the Continent in the latter part of the nineteenth century, have no definite position for each couple in relation to the other couples."[39]

Twenty years later on, at dances in the 1940s, young Dudley Laufman encountered a wide mix of polkas, waltzes, square dances, Broadway show tunes, French-Canadian reels, and Irish jigs. A few

---

38. From the Square Dance History website https://squaredancehistory.org courtesy of David Millstone.

39. Eloise Hubbard Linscott, *Folk Songs of Early New England* (New York: Dover Publications, 1990), 58.

old contras like "Hull's Victory" and "Chorus Jig" were scattered around in a typical dance playlist of "Ain't She Sweet," "When Irish Eyes Are Smiling," "Shine On Harvest Moon," and scores of other standard tunes that had been preserved in popular memory. The regional landscape was splashed with a lively spectrum of local color in granges, church basements, and dance halls were still scattered throughout New England after V-J Day. Much would depend upon the caller and the musicians, but the basic flavor came from the core identity and personality of the dancers. In places in Massachusetts like the Franco-American Hall in Chicopee and Hibernian Hall in Dudley Square in Boston, in New Hampshire at the Ukrainian-American Club in Manchester and Huggins Barn in Tamworth, or over in Maine at halls like the Blue Goose in Northport and the Locke Mill Grange in Greenwood, local culture and local preferences ruled. At Benson's Barn up in Saxton's River, Vermont, the all-night dance was kept alive for years. Dancers and musicians convened in the evening and kept things rolling until dawn's early light, when it was time to go back home and milk the cows.

A strong tradition of musicians "sitting in" was an established practice in New England, and it allowed Dudley and his contemporaries to play with many good dance bands. Dozens of callers worked throughout the region and were remembered fondly by dancers and musicians alike. The affable Joe Perkins called dances in a circuit on the North Shore (Salem, Topsfield, and Rockport), and he let Dudley join in on harmonica. A postmaster from the South Shore named Charles Baldwin was a singing caller who played on Wednesdays at the Boston YMCA, another genial dance leader who had Dudley sit in. Ted Sannella, a native of Revere, was a popular and friendly caller; early on, Dudley remembers playing "Lamplighter's Hornpipe" at one of his dances on piano and harmonica. Ted called at dances in Porter Square, down at Westport Point, and in North Whitefield, Maine, where he lived in his later years. Sylvia Miskoe of Concord, New Hampshire, sat in with both the Ralph Page and Duke Miller orchestras, and with Louise Winston, who called square dances in Jamaica Plain. Ms. Winston once grabbed the hem of

Sylvia Miskoe's skirt and hauled it down to what she considered to be a decent latitude.

Folks out at the Circle 9 Ranch in Epsom duded up in western shirts or fringed skirts, cowboy boots, and red bandannas, dancing in squares to "The Trail of the Lonesome Pine," while up at the Tunbridge Fair dancers were stepping out in old-time top hats, satin dresses, and tails to the strains of "Soldier's Joy." Over at Bell's Studio in Peterborough, Ralph Page's boys dressed neatly in chinos and sport coats, Dick Richardson in a dark dress shirt and a white necktie, Bob McQuillen in a neat plaid flannel shirt. The band was ready to jump into anything from "Red River Valley" to the old "Glise A Sherbrooke" and have a fine time doing it.[40] Dudley was throwing his lot in with an aging art form, but one that still had a staunch and a lively group of adherents spread throughout New England.

Tradition, certainly, was the guiding force behind the thousand-year-old line of country dancing, but so was the innovation of creative and strong-minded musicians, dancers, and callers. Ed Larkin of Tunbridge, Vermont, called dances while he played the fiddle. Happy Hale of Bernardston, Massachusetts, once said "Sometimes I think up real good changes of my own—and then, first chance I get, I try 'em out!" Hale's key innovation was singing while he was calling—Ralph Page heard him do that at "the Springfield Fair"[41] and took the practice on as his own. Old Edson Cole of Ossipee, New Hampshire, one of the earliest callers and fiddlers we have on recordings, told Eloise Linscott, "You can play them any way you've a mind to, but even though I learned my tunes from Uncle Jim, *I've got a yank of my own.*"[42] For independent minded traditionalists

---

40. Sources for more information include Ralph Page and Beth Tolman's *The Country Dance Book* (New York: Barnes & Co., 1937) and the Smithsonian Folkways CD *Choose Your Partner* (SFW CD 40126) including extensive notes by Jack Beard, Lynne Martin, and Kate Van Winkle Keller.

41. Up-country reference to the Eastern States Exposition, one of the largest agricultural fairs in New England.

42. Eloise Hubbard Linscott, *Folk Songs of Early New England* (New York: Dover Publications,1990), 59.

like Dudley Laufman and the bright, capable musicians who joined forces with him in the Canterbury Country Dance Orchestra in the 1960s, this sort of an approach was music to the ears. There was a strong tradition living on in all these tunes, yet that musical inheritance was in the hands of the holder as well as the beholder. The measure of a good evening was in the sum total of heritage and improvisation that sprang to life in the dance.

On a warm spring evening in the late 1940s, a "Caller's Jamboree" was convened at the Concord, New Hampshire, high school. The dozens of country dance callers, musicians, and dancers who attended were among the very best in the business. Dudley, Ted Sannella, and Larry Collins hitchhiked up from Massachusetts, and after a first-rate dance, Bob McQuillen invited folks to stay overnight at his place in sleeping bags out in the field. Next morning, after a hearty breakfast, the musicians unlimbered their instruments and all began playing again.

Dudley remembers that Bob placed a telephone call to the local high school, spoke with a music teacher, and suggested that they send a few student-musicians over to sit in with the gathering of veterans. "They arrived and listened to such tunes as they had never heard before…Devil's Dream, Old Joe Clark, and Peter Street," remembers Dudley. "Afterwards Bob told the kids, 'Don't bother to go back to school, boys, just go swimming.'"[43]

---

43. Callers in attendance included Gene Gowing, Ralph Page, Ted Sannella, Al Brundage, Hal Brundage, Larry Loy, Pop Smith, and Ed Durlacher. Musicians included George Gulyassy, Bob Gulyassy, Dick Best, Dick Richardson, Russ Allen, Bob McQuillen, Johnny Tremblay, Junior Richardson, and Norm Smith. From the Dudley Laufman entry on the Ted Sannella memory page of the Monadnock Folklore Society website.

≡ 6 ≡

The Old Hinterlands of
Vermont and Massachusetts

I N 1939, KENNETH AND SUSAN HOARD WEBB founded a summer
program in the hills outside of Plymouth, Vermont, that they
named the Farm and Wilderness Camps. The organization was
philosophically based upon the thought and work of John Dewey,
and it continues to successfully operate as "a system of accredited
Quaker-based summer camps for kids and summer programs
for teens rooted in social justice, environmental sustainability,
homegrown fun, and wilderness adventure." The camps attracted a
loyal clientele that both enjoyed and believed in the outdoor living
and progressive idealism that combined in a creative calendar of
summer events. Through friends, Dudley learned that the position
of farm manager was available at the Vermont camp. He filled out an
application, and he got the job.

The spring of 1951 came late, and there was deep mud in
the roads and three feet of snow still lay in the woods when young
Dudley Laufman ventured up to Farm and Wilderness Camp and
took up residence as Farm Manager. He was driven up to a remote
cabin and dropped off near the home of his closest neighbors, the
Terwiligers, where he was to get his meals. That spring, he pulled
the farm together, bringing the camp's Jersey dairy cattle back home
from where they had been boarded at a nearby farm, tending to

chores, and surviving an incident where he rolled the camp jeep off the narrow dirt road and down into the woods.

The open nature of a summer camp program like Farm and Wilderness could tend to operate far outside the realities of the agricultural "life style" that, at least in theory, it espoused. With a hay crop cut, cured, and ready to be brought into the barn, Dudley might have discovered that the farm truck had suddenly been commandeered to carry a bunch of canoes over to a nearby lake. A labor force of young arms that had been expected to help with the harvest might have been kited off to climb a mountain or to go for a swim. The obligations of the farm year did not come to a sudden close when the sheets on the bunkbeds were stripped after Labor Day; agricultural tasks had to be tended to well into the month of October. The young farm manager saw that somebody had to settle down to brass tacks and get the work done. Necessary adjustments were eventually arrived at.

At Farm and Wilderness, Dudley met Jack Sloanaker of Belmont, Massachusetts, a Harvard-trained psychologist who served as a director at the camp, and who was also an avid folk dancer and a skilled and a dedicated musician. Jack regularly played at dances in Boston and in Cambridge, applying the background of his classical training to the lively idiom of contradance. Like Dudley, Jack was a convinced convert to the old art form, a heart-and-soul true believer in the old music. At Farm and Wilderness, he arranged for campers to go up to a dance that was held regularly at Sherburne Center, Vermont, a small town located between Woodstock and Rutland. He introduced Dudley to Lin Cady, the local singing caller whose group had played at the 1925 Presidential inauguration of Plymouth, Vermont native Calvin Coolidge.[44]

Eventually, Jack decided that instead of traveling to Sherburne Center it would be better to hold dances at Farm and Wilderness, and he enlisted Dudley as caller and accordion player, joining in

---

44. Cady's group included his wife on piano, Ken Terwiliger on saxophone, and a banjo, a fiddle, and an accordion.

himself on bass and banjo. Over time, Jack began to organize and teach a group of young campers in what became known as the F&W String Band. Very rapidly, Dudley's life was becoming defined by farming and square dancing. He was regularly attending dances at Sherburne Center and at F&W in Vermont, at Nelson in New Hampshire, in Boston at the Ralph Page evenings at the Boston "Y" on Clarendon Street, and in other venues. He also began traveling down to Chicopee, Massachusetts, where a lively dance was regularly held at the Franco-American Hall.

In 1951, Dudley enrolled at the Stockbridge School of Agriculture at the University of Massachusetts in Amherst. Stockbridge had been at the core of the UMass program since its founding as a land-grant college in 1863. The curriculum included courses in animal husbandry, dairy farming, poultry production, horticulture, arboriculture, pomology, and turf management. Stockbridge graduates have gone on to own and manage farms throughout New England, and the program remains vital and influential to this day. The formal education gleaned at the Norfolk Agriculture School and then at the Stockbridge School became the foundation of knowledge that Dudley applied at Farm and Wilderness Camp, and then later on at the Walpole, New Hampshire, farm of G. Allan Holmes, where he was employed for a time.

In the wake of World War II and "the Korean conflict," the government had instituted a universal peacetime draft system to which young men were required to register at age eighteen. When they graduated from high school or college, they were expected to serve a term of two years of military duty in one of the branches of the armed services. Most draftees spent a year or so in the United States Army unless they could qualify for an academic exemption or a medical deferment. Many young working-class high school graduates would go to work for a contractor, a mover, or trucking company until they were called up by the draft board, and then off they went to boot camp and a thirteen-month stint in Europe or the Far East. In every small town in New England, young veterans in their mid-twenties could fill you in on what life was like on a military base in Germany, or who, on a Saturday night, came to town in silk aviator jackets embroidered with the image of a colorful dragon and the name "Korea."

Draftees could request a conscientious objector deferment, asking to be exempted from military service due to their religious objections to war. If the local draft board approved such a request, a young man would be required to provide twenty-four months of "alternative service" in a low-paying job, usually in a menial position at a hospital. Later on, during the Vietnam era, this would become a widespread course of action, but in the early 1950s, it was an unusual option to pursue. Not uncharacteristically, this was the course Dudley Laufman chose in 1953.

Dudley could readily base his case on Quaker beliefs, and that he did, but he is also quick, these days, to simply assert that the idea of putting himself in a position to be shot full of holes was a non-starter for him on practical as well as moral terms. He was granted the CO status after an interview in which the draft board seemed mainly interested in talking about the prospects of the Boston Red Sox.

When Dudley was required to decide where he would perform his alternate service, he made the choice based solely on his desire to keep on contradancing. In order to continue traversing through the constellation of New England dance locations, he accepted a job as an orderly at Brattleboro Retreat, a private psychiatric facility founded in 1834 and located on a six-hundred-acre campus situated just west of the Connecticut River, not far from Farm and Wilderness Camp. Alternate service jobs were designed to be difficult as well as low-paying. As an orderly on the noon-to-midnight shift, Dudley was subjected to an unwanted dose of hardship. "It was horrible," he remembers. "I had to wear a white uniform with a bow tie, and I worked in really rough conditions." In such situations, a mental health orderly was not much more than a combined security guard, janitor, changer of soiled clothing, nurse's aide, and custodian. The patients were low-functioning and were often aggressive, the conditions were daunting, and the routine was emotionally traumatic. The lifeline away from the locked ward became an old Model A Ford that spirited Dudley away to dances in Amherst, in Brattleboro, in the Boston area, or to the little town hall over in Nelson, New Hampshire.[45]

---

45. Nelson was incorporated in 1774 as Packersfield, named after the sheriff of Portsmouth. On April 20, 1775, twenty-seven men from town marched to Cambridge "at the Lexington alarm."

Nelson and the New England Contradance Tradition

IN THE LATE 1700s, COUNTRY DANCING had been a social art form that thrived in thousands of parlors and dance halls in hundreds of cities and towns between the St. Lawrence and Long Island Sound. But by about the time of the Civil War, the old tunes had begun to retreat to backwater enclaves in rural Maine, in the foothills of the White Mountains, in the Monadnock region of New Hampshire, and in hamlets tucked amongst the hills of old Vermont. The traditions that had started coming over the water in the 1600s remained vigorous, but by the 1950s, for the most part, they were in the hands of past-keepers who were fast approaching their Biblical allotment of three score years and ten. Folklorist Eloise Hubbard Linscott (1897–1978) began collecting tunes and songs throughout rural New England, encouraged by Alan Lomax and given direction and support from poet Archibald MacLeish, who had been appointed by Franklin Roosevelt in 1939 to be the head of the Library of Congress. By 1940, Linscott was recording a broad variety of traditional musicians, from members of the Passamaquoddy tribe of Dana Point, Maine, to retired sea captains on the Massachusetts coast. Fiddlers and callers whose work she added to the library included Happy Hale of Bernardston, Massachusetts; Edson Cole and Arthur Hanson of Ossipee, New Hampshire; Langdon Ambrose of Sandwich, New Hampshire; Carrie Grover of Gorham, Maine; Willie Woodward of Bristol, New Hampshire; Arthur Walden and George "Rocky Mountain" Brown of Tamworth, New Hampshire; and the New Hampshire Guides Band, among many others.[46]

Vermont fiddler and maple producer Ed Larkin was recorded by Linscott and in 1941 was photographed by Jack Delano of the Federal Works Project Administration at the Tunbridge Fair. Old Ed was still going strong then and he would continue to do so until 1954, but he'd been born on Christmas Day in 1867, and like a good number of the other regional fiddlers and callers he hearkened far back into the nineteenth century.[47] In the early 1950s, Dudley Laufman was an enthusiastic young acolyte in what was very rapidly becoming an old man's game. By his teens and early twenties, Dudley was drawing deeply from the well of New England contradance tradition. His youthful wanderings took him into a realm where the faith was still being kept in the era of homespun and hornpipes.

The old town of Nelson, New Hampshire, had been among the many remote points on Eloise Linscott's folkloric compass. By the 1950s, the town was a peaceful and very much out-of-the-way place where artistic talent and Yankee culture came together in a natural course of informal human events. Nobody gave a seminar and nobody called a committee meeting. In 2004, videographer Paul Tuller sat down with old-timers Frank Upton, Renn Tolman, and Dudley Laufman to record a sense of Nelson's unique qualities and its function as a creative, tradition-based place:

Dudley Laufman: "Until about seventy-five years ago, I would say… the kind of dancing that we do in this region, the traditional dancing, was not done outside of this area. And so what fascinates me is, why did this place have a handle on it?"

---

46. Linscott was working in a rural atmosphere that very much "still had the bark on it." One of her informants referred to his autoharp as a "mountain piano."

47. Ed Larkin's work and memory have been kept alive in the Ed Larkin Dancers, who still convene in top hats and gowns every year in Tunbridge.

Frank Upton: "I always wondered about that...but of course, everyone knows it's true! If you go back to any historian who knows anything about square dancing...it's Nelson square dancing, you know..."

Dudley Laufman: "I think it has a lot to do with the isolation of the area. There's no major highway moving in or out...and a lot of times French-Canadian, Irish, and Scottish people living here have contributed, and then the wealthy that came here in the summer because of the lake...twenty miles up the road from here, in Hillsborough, they don't talk about this..."

Renn Tolman: "But what actually happened is you had a combination of people who came together, Newt and Fran and Quig, and a few others who knew these old dances that sort of had died out...and it was Ralph Page and one thing or another who revived old dances around here, and they were the old dances that they remembered...that's basically what happened..."

Dudley Laufman: "It was like snowballing..."[48]

The idiosynchractic Tolman family had lived in Nelson in the shadow of Mount Monadnock since the 1700s. Newt Tolman (1908–1986) played classical flute and his brother Fran (1902–1969) the piano, and they invited a gifted painter, Albert Quigley (1891–1961), to join them on the fiddle and work out arrangements to some of the old-time contradance numbers. As the story goes, the trio were playing one night in a disused cider mill and had invited Ralph Page (1903–1985) to listen in on the session; Page began calling traditional dance calls in time to their music. One thing led to another, including the purchase of an old Model A Ford sedan, in which the Ralph Page group began touring to preside at dances throughout the Monadnock region and its environs, all the way to Boston.

---

48. From The Nelson History Group, 2004; nelson.org. Paul Tuller of Dublin was the videographer. These videos are hosted on the Monadnock Folklore Society You Tube Channel.

Frank Upton: "Quig had the car, and Ralph was a miserable tight-fisted old cuss, never owned an auto*mo*bile in his life, never learned to drive. So Quig had to drive him to Boston, two or three nights a week to play. And they had to drive all over… Quig…like many others around here, never paid attention to a *bud*get…Ralph, one night, coming home from Boston, they'd played at a dance down there for some rich people, and Quig was going to get his fifteen dollars, which was a lot of money in those days. And on the way home Ralph started preachin' to Quig about how to budget. How to *live*…'You want to take half of it, put it in the bank. We play at these dances…maybe you can skim a little off, build up a little account…and if you have some stormy weather…when we don't have a couple of dances, then you'll have a little something to fall back on.' And he preached all the way back from Boston about this and they got home. Quig hadn't said a word. And Ralph said, 'What do you think, Quig, what I had to say?' And Quig said, 'Well, there's a lot of ways you live that I don't like either, Ralph.' And that was the end of it!"

Volumes, or at least chapters, could be written about each of these good people, but the collective story revolves around Page, who was born just outside of Keene and who sprang forth from lines of ancestral Irish minstrels, dance callers, and at least one fiddler. In December of 1930, Ralph was playing the fiddle at a dance when the caller's voice seized up and he was asked to pinch hit. He never stopped calling. By 1937, he was co-writing *The Country Dance Book* with Beth Tolman, wherein, among many other things, he expounded on the idea that the revival of country dance was "the first crocus in the recovery of civilization from its self-poisoning."[49]

---

49. Page cited the following as the guiding principles of the idiom: Community, Individualism, Pliability, Feeling for the Past, Forward-Looking, Robustness (as opposed to degeneration), Democracy, Skill and Control, Employment, Tolerance ("good neighbor policy") and Freedom. Ralph Page and Beth Tolman, *The Country Dance Book* (New York: Barnes & Co., 1937), 23–25.

In 1939, Page led the traditional dances at the New York World's Fair. In 1943, he began holding weekly square and contradances at the Boston YWCA on Clarendon Street, often backed up by Ed Koenig on fiddle, Hayden Sweat on bass, and Cy Kano on piano. Musicians and dancers convened in the chandeliered, balconied second-floor ballroom at a gig where Ralph presided for a quarter-century. In 1946, he was a founder of the New England Folk Festival, which quickly became a port of call for traditional musicians from throughout the region. Page was chosen by the U.S. State Department to be a goodwill ambassador for America, touring England, Russia, and Japan. He began a series of folk-dance camps in New England, compiled and edited 165 issues of his *Northern Junket* magazine, and wrote extensively on contradance practice and traditions in the books *Heritage Dances of Early America, An Elegant Collection of Contras and Squares,* and *The Ralph Page Book of Contras.* In addition, he recorded dances, music, and calls on Moses Asch's *Disc* records and Michael Herman's *Folk Dancer* label.[50]

Ralph Page may have been among the first contradance leaders who concentrated on both a defining "sound" to his music and a "tone" to the dance proceedings that amounted to his signatures. He borrowed the idea of being a "singing caller" from old "Happy" Hale of Bernardston, Massachusetts, who had danced and called so enthusiastically that the trove of cigars in his jacket pocket often ended up rolling around under the feet of the dancers on the floor. Page owed much to a choice of excellent musicians whose sound blended into a characteristic musical personality. He saw to it that a Ralph Page dance was very much the result of a unique convention of his tastes and a team of first-rate talents who knew each other's styles as thoroughly as they knew the old material. He referred to

---

50. Page's Folk Dancer records were released on Michael Herman's characteristic red-and-yellow Folk Dancer Record Service label. The Disc release was a three 78 rpm folio set that featured an improbable cover illustration of several women dressed in gauzy costumes. Clearly a big city creation, a case of bronchitis would have been the result if that sort of an ethereal outfit would have ever been worn in a New Hampshire dance hall.

his musical mixture with characteristic pithiness as "precision and imagination." He also relied upon dancers who knew their business: "perfectly average looking people of mostly oldish years, fat and thin, tall and squat…just a neighborly group getting together for a whirl. It would be hard to describe how *good* these people were…"[51]

Ralph's dances had a personality that very much sprang from his own tastes and preferences. As he put it in a letter to *Folk Dancer's* Michael Herman, "I think that most of the international dances are grand and the tunes and figures delightful, but because of my background I specialize in the American dance and keep the others as a sideline. Throughout the years I have come to appreciate both types of folk dances more and more. One other thing—I insist on my sessions being clean and wholesome. I will not tolerate drunkenness or rowdyism. I let people have a good time, you understand, but there is a difference between a good time and a brawl."[52] Ralph Page was very much a gentleman as well as being something of a raconteur, inserting entertaining asides, greetings to old acquaintances, and colorful comments into his calls and introductions. Although their personalities and experiences were quite different, the distinctive styles and the "stamp" of individuality in performance very much charcterized the life work of both the elder Ralph Page and the impressionable young Dudley Laufman.

Monday night came the dance at the Nelson Town Hall, Tuesday at the Boston "Y," and the rest of the calendar was a catch-as-catch-can mix of shindigs held nearly every evening somewhere in eastern and central New England.[53] For the musicians, this could represent as steady a source of cash as could be found during

---

51. Ralph Page and Beth Tolman, *The Country Dance Book* (New York: Barnes & Co., 1937), 183–184.

52. *Folk Dancer*, Vol. 6, No. 1, January 1946.

53. In addition to Page and Hale, prominent dance callers of the period included Ted Sannella of Concord, Massachusetts, Duke Miller, Charlie Webster, Dave Fuller, Johnny Trafton, Jim Morrison, and Ted Glabach, among many others.

the Depression days. On a weekly basis, an improvised roster of musicians were convened as opportunities presented themselves and as availability dictated. On any given night, a caller had to "line up" a roster of instrumentalists who could create enough of a "sound" to carry a dance. The vicissitudes of personality, transportation, and weather all resolved themselves as soon as the words "Honor your partner, bow to your corner" were intoned into a microphone that approximated the size of a quart bottle of milk, or maybe were just bellowed out over the crowd sounds into the teeming bee-hive of an old-fashioned dance hall.

For a band as good as Ralph Page's was, the sum of the parts told the story. Johnny Tremblay provided a solid, consistent foundation on the piano, and Junior Richardson pushed the rhythm along on his big stand-up bass. Bob McQuillen's rich piano accordion provided blanket chording and stirring melody by turn, allowing the twin fiddles of the sturdy veteran Dick Richardson and the facile young Russ Allen to soar up together above the lot. Page sang his calls in a rich tenor, his Yankee accent sounding authoritative and yet neighborly at the same time. This was the core group that curated the contradance tradition into the twentieth century from the Ed Larkins, Happy Hales, and Edson Coles who had, in their own times, grown up hearing echoes from back in the early 1800s. Whatever else you could say about them, the old country dances certainly seemed to foster a remarkable degree of longevity among their callers.[54]

---

54. Ralph Page, who was born in 1903, remembered his grandmother telling him of an aged fiddler named Wilson who, when "Hull's Victory" was being played, insisted on wearing "an old, forlorn seersucker coat which he said he'd been wearing when the news came of the victory of Hull's *Constitution*" in the summer of 1812. Page and Tolman, *The Country Dance Book*, p. 89.

⇒ 8 ⇐

Pilgrimage to Canterbury

THE TWO-YEAR TERM OF DUDLEY LAUFMAN'S mandatory conscientious objector service ended in August of 1955, very likely the longest and possibly the only part of his adult life that was severely constrained by outside forces. He celebrated his freedom by going to dinner with friends in Brattleboro, then drove directly to the Gilford, Vermont, town hall to play for a dance there. The next morning, he had coffee in Nelson with his friend Frankie Upton. Then, with his Model A Ford loaded with everything he owned, he drove to Hillsborough, New Hampshire, to take a job "doing heavy work" at the Hillsboro Camp for girls run by Mrs. Harry Nissen, who was known to everyone as Aunt Jane. Dudley immediately took up a long roster of duties: chopping and splitting wood, chipping ice, fixing canoes, making ice cream, feeding and caring for the camp's horses, and "playing tennis and flirting with all the girls." The job filled the week except for Saturday nights, which were spent playing for the dance at Nelson Town Hall.[55]

As the days shortened, he prepped the camp for winter, did odd jobs and carpentry for Aunt Jane Nissen, repaired an old bridge,

---

55. A representative playlist from a Nelson dance of the period included: "Money Musk," "Morning Star," "Chorus Jig," "Lady Walpole's Reel," "Hull's Victory," and "Petronella."

patched up a roof with Frank Upton, chopped wood, and began writing poetry and prose. He dated a local schoolteacher, skied at Mount Sunapee, cut ice, shoveled snow off the camp roofs, and served for a time as scoutmaster of the Hillsborough Boy Scout Troop 73. The long winter full of blizzards turned into sugar season, and in April, with four feet of snow still in the woods, he tapped out and set 120 buckets in Aunt Jane's sugar bush and went to boiling maple syrup. One memorable day Frank Upton came over to help, bearing with him an ample supply of good old hard cider, which he and Dudley "got into," as the saying goes. Soon thereafter, on a Sunday morning, Dudley lugged a portable Webcor reel-to-reel tape recorder over to the Tolman Farm and recorded four sprightly old contradance tunes with Newt and Renn Tolman on flutes, Albert Quigley on fiddle, and himself on accordion.[56] With that job done, he stopped in Dublin to visit with Bob McQuillen before having a mug of hot chocolate and driving home.

Even as he was enjoying the fellowship of these extraordinary people, Dudley began to experience a deep restlessness. He began reading Byron, Shelley, and Trelawney, and he described in a letter to his brother Alan how the character of those men's lives intrigued him even more than their writing did. He began to feel, as he put it, a "passion to be like these different people," yet at times he could interpret this interest as a sort of character weakness. How was a young man in his mid-20s supposed to interpret the forces that beguiled him in the direction of the ancient realm of rural dance during the very weeks in 1956 that millions of other youths across the United States were being hypnotized by the wail of Elvis Presley singing his new RCA Victor hit "Heartbreak Hotel"?

Dudley Laufman married Cynthia Dunbar of Chester, New Hampshire, in 1957, and the young couple took up housekeeping in a fifth-floor walkup behind the New Hampshire State Library in Concord. With his alternate service behind him, Dudley went

---

56. "Ross's Reel #4," "Batchelder's Reel," "Durang's Hornpipe," and "Speed the Plow."

about the business of making enough of a living to keep body, soul, inspiration, and a young family together. He took a job as activities director at the New Hampshire State Hospital, organizing softball and basketball games for the more active residents. For the sedentary storytellers, he would play songs like "Home On The Range" and "Bicycle Built for Two" on what he referred to as his "humungous Lawrence Welk piano accordion."

There at the state hospital he met Arthur Hanson of Ossipee, an old-time fiddler who, long before, had been one of Eloise Linscott's sources. As a youth, when Hanson finished playing at dances over in Parsonsfield, Maine, he lay down in his buggy and fell asleep, trusting his horse to take him the twenty miles home over across the state line. One hot July day, the old man interrupted Dudley's rendition of "Jingle Bells" to ask if he knew "Soldier's Joy" and several other old-time fiddle tunes. Of course he did! The old man introduced himself, saying "My name is Arthur Hanson and I used to play the fiddle before I came here." He soon produced an ancient instrument and began playing "Haste To the Wedding." The two men went on sharing the old tunes all afternoon, running through their conjoined repertoires and having a wonderful time. Thus began a long friendship. The young man brought the old man out from the hospital to play for dances in small towns throughout New Hampshire. Eventually, Arthur Hanson asked Dudley that when the time came, he would help see to it that he was laid to rest in his family plot in the woods up in Ossipee. Later on, that is what came to pass. A social worker of Dudley's acquaintance spoke with the local selectmen and saw to the necessary arrangements. Dudley played a few venerable tunes over Arthur's grave with his friend Taylor Whiteside, bowing the fiddle that the old timer had left to him, and which Dudley has played ever since.[57]

New Hampshire was not the only place where people were dancing to a different fiddle in the early 1950s, and contradancers

---

57. For the whole story, be sure to scout out Dudley's recording "Jacket Trimmed In Blue." Bring a handkerchief.

were only one strain of Yankees who kept one foot in a different century. The idea of non-conformists living out in the woods was not a foreign concept in the North Country. There was hardly a rural town in New England that didn't have a hermit "batchin' it" in a remote camp out on a disused old road, living on venison, trout, and turnips, with a daughter-in-law or the town cop bringing out a box of groceries once in a while. Some were old men, and some old women; Robert Frost wrote poems about a few of each. Some were socialists, and at least one die-hard Republican imbedded a shiny new dime into the hardwood of his threshold so he could tread on the image of the architect of the New Deal while coming and going from his woodshed. Non-conformity of the 1950s and 1960s in rural New England had a creative yet traditional strain of underlying libertarianism about it. It was nomadic but it had oriented itself in the direction of hearth and homestead. It was independent and yet it valued community. At its best, it knew enough to be ready to listen and to learn. At its most successful, it respected a native reverence for individuality; it minded its own business. Above all else, it sought to meet the gold standard of Yankee integrity, as expressed in the phrase, "Well, I can see that you hain't afraid of hard work!"

Among the more famous, or at least the better-published fugitive agrarians, was Scott Nearing, a one-time professor of economics at the Wharton School who, in the words of his biographer, "voyaged to the wilderness as if on a pilgrimage to a sacred place."[58] In 1954, after homesteading for two decades on an abandoned hill farm in Jamaica, Vermont, Nearing and his wife Helen published a book on self-sufficiency that they titled *Living the Good Life*. The volume attracted little attention at the time, although a generation later it would become a best-seller. While he was still at Farm and Wilderness, Dudley had pilgrimed up the road to Jamaica, Vermont, with a friend to pay a visit to the farm site that the Nearings had deeded over free and clear to the town before heading over to the coast of

---

58. John A. Saltmarsh, *Scott Nearing: An Intellectual Biography* (Philadelphia: Temple University Press, 1991), 2–3.

Maine. Much as in the role he played with contradances, Dudley was a raindrop in a trickle of rural idiosyncrasy that over time would grow to a torrent in the "back to the land" movement of the late 1960s. But such things were yet unheard of in the Eisenhower years. In New Hampshire, if someone wanted to live out in the woods it was their own G.D. business.

About this time, as she had been on many other occasions, Dudley's mother played the role of *dea ex machina* in her son's life. Not, this time, by giving birth or taking him to his first dance in Nelson, but by suggesting that he might drop in on the Quaker meeting in the old town of Canterbury, just north of Concord. And so indeed he did, discovering that along with silent Quakers, the town was home to celibate Shakers, sweet maple syrup makers, tart apple pickers, an alternative school named Horizon's Edge, an outspoken teetotaler whose son would later grow up to run a distillery in a barn upon her property, and a local teacher and homesteader who was working on a book about the Holocaust that eventually would win him a National Jewish Book Award.[59] It was a typical New Hampshire town.

A landowner named David Curtis put pen to paper in 1957 and for $25 signed a deed over to Dudley for two acres of pasture land on Shaker Road. For another $900, the young man bought a supply of used timbers and boards from a dismantled Lutheran vestry building in Concord sufficient to erect a homemade house that he named "Wind in the Timothy." He moved with his wife Cynthia and their little daughter Heidi into a community he once described as full of people who "lived in the woods, smelled of wood smoke, and were their own bosses." The couple began to grow their own food in rich soil bordering the Shaker Village that had been under skilled cultivation for more than two centuries. Within a few years, Dudley and Cynthia ventured up to spend a week visiting with the Nearings in Maine. Three more children arrived: Bronwen, Nathaniel, and Singwen. Like many, if not most, in town, the family

---

59. David Sword Wyman, *The Abandonment of the Jews: America and the Holocaust, 1941–1945* (New York: Pantheon Books, 1984).

ate the food they had harvested and stayed warm all winter burning wood that Dudley had cut and split by hand near their home place. He continued to play at dances every week in Nelson. On stormy winter days, he squeezed the notes on the accordion by the glowing stove as the wind whistled west across the pasture and the snow blew up against the clear, red, blue, and gold diamond-paned windows of the little farmstead.

Change was just over the horizon. In retrospect, we can see what might have not been visible at the time, that a spontaneous, creative surge in traditional music was taking place throughout the New England region. Eric von Schmidt was the catalyst for a blues and folk revival in Cambridge while Jim Rooney and Bill Keith served the same role in bluegrass and old-timey music in Amherst. At the University of Massachusetts, Buffy Sainte-Marie was becoming a singer-songwriter and Taj Mahal was performing in a rhythm and blues band. A core of excellent country dance musicians was gathering loosely around Nelson, Brattleboro, Amherst, Franconia, and other compass points in New England. Traditional dancers gathered weekly at various points in Cambridge and Boston including the Friday night Porter Square dances called by Ted Sannella, which Sylvia Miskoe remembers as "three squares, a contra, and an international dance." At the University of New Hampshire in Durham, young Sylvia joined a group of dancers that convened and called themselves "the Durham Reelers." Music histories focus readily on instrumentalists and their personalities, yet the tradition could not have existed or been kept alive if there had not been a solid bedrock of enthusiastic couples who took joy in the many forms of country dance. The heart of the matter played out on the worn wooden floors of the dance halls. When she is asked about the beginnings of her long and noteworthy career as one of the leading traditional musicians in New England, Sylvia Miskoe answers quickly and simply: "I have *always* loved to dance!"[60]

---

60. Author's interview with Sylvia Miskoe, Concord, New Hampshire, 5/6/22.

In a modern era that may be more prone to analyze traditional art more readily than to enjoy it, it is good to recall how eclectic and un-self-conscious the old country dances could be. At a hall in Bradford, New Hampshire, called Fortune's Barn, folks would gather on a Saturday night and enjoy a variety of dance styles. The evening might begin with a square dance like "Nellie Bly," or "Golden Slippers," then move into a fox trot danced, perhaps, to a popular swing band tune, then step into a waltz (the "Tennessee Waltz" is a good example).[61] Just before intermission, the band might launch into "Irish Washerwoman." Each of these dances ended with applause, bowing, and clapping. Intermission would be followed by the remainder of the dances for the evening, mostly squares, interspersed with fox-trots, polkas, and waltzes. All this made for a lively event, with the old-timers getting a chance to catch up with friends and the young people having the opportunity to preen, flirt, and strut their stuff on the dance floor. Nobody actually said out loud, as people sometimes did at African-American dance clubs, "Let me see what you got!" but that's only because they were Yankees.

There was an enormous vitality in the old-time country dance culture of New England. Dance was an opportunity to express one's physical sense of self, publicly and spontaneously, in a community of like-minded individuals. Personalities and ego are all part of the human condition and all came into play in the dynamics of an evening of dance. Yet, unlike daily life in an office building, a faculty lounge, or a beauty parlor, an emotional consensus usually prevails through the craft of the music and the joy of the dance once the tunes began. When the well-known strains of "Darling Nelly Grey" began, seasoned dancers would know the drill. First couple to the right and balance the two. Elbows bent, make a neat step swing balance. Step

---

61. A popular tune for generations, and a beautiful one, but the author can't help but remember the thoughts of an old French-Canadian carpenter from Tilton who scorned the song's sentimental account of a best friend stealing the singer's sweetheart at a dance: "What a bunch of bullshit. I would have punched the crap out of him right out on the dance floor."

on right foot, pass left foot over across in front of right, knees bent just a bit, then right foot across left, maybe with just a hint of a pigeon wing, then an easy shuffle two step, circle, then right and left and off you go.[62] As Levon Helm once said about playing the drums, "It's easy when you know how!"

This was the world in which the youthful Dudley Laufman, late of the corner of Pleasant and Gould in Arlington, found himself. He was, by all accounts, a good-looking young man who readily drew and welcomed the attention of women. Yet he was also a growing-up version of a kid who hadn't fit in completely in his home town. His family were Quakers, which immediately set them apart from the conventional Massachusetts mix of Catholic parishes and Protestant congregations. In the midst of the insecure suburban world of class and status, he had been irrevocably relegated to the "slow" class as a youth. Largely acting on his own, Dudley had developed odd, rural tastes and archaic musical inclinations. At the farm in Fremont and later in the town hall in Nelson, he had seen a bit of a rip in the fabric of fate and he had chosen to stride straight through it towards the sound of a fiddle. All of a sudden he was not an outlier; he had stumbled across a perfectly intuitive seed-bed for his life's work. The world of country dance was a heady mix of lively traditions, and Dudley soaked them all up, arriving at the dance halls like a young musical wizard with his accordion slung picturesquely over his shoulder and perhaps an old tune in his head:

> *I am a fiddler to my trade*
> *And all the tunes that e'er I played,*
> *The sweetest still to wife or maid,*
> *Was whistle o'er the love of it....*

By virtue of his broad itinerary, his charismatic personality, and a soul-deep identification with the country dance idiom, Dudley began to draw superb musicians into a vortex around him. Early

---

62. Dudley Laufman entry on Ted Sannella memory page of the Monadnock Folklore Society website.

on, he played accordion and harmonica in a holder and called the dances, often accompanied by Sylvia Miskoe of Concord on accordion, Joe Ryan of Northfield on fiddle, and Bob McQuillen of Dublin or Kay Gilbert of Nelson on piano. On any given night and venue, Newt Tolman might arrive with his flute, ready to soar above the ensemble, Jack O'Connor might provide the anchor on bass, Dave Fuller might join in on accordion, and some combination of Vince O'Donnell, Ted Levin, Jerry Weene, Nicholas Howe, and Allan Block might be wielding the fiddles. Peter Colby would play either banjo or autoharp on instruments of his own custom design and construction.[63]

Vince O'Donnell was an accomplished jazz and classical musician, a native of Philadelphia who had come north to attend Harvard graduate school. A young man of strong convictions, he had spent much of the eventful summer of 1964 working on behalf of the Civil Rights Movement at the campus of Tugaloo College in Jackson, Mississippi. Three counties away, FBI agents were digging up the bodies of slain activists Andrew Goodman, James Chaney, and Michael Schwerner. The following year, Vince's wife met Dudley Laufman at an American Friends Service Committee Meeting that was held in New Hampshire. Dudley invited her and Vince to a poetry reading and music session to be held in Canterbury.

Vince remembers taking the bus up from Boston to Concord, New Hampshire, and then somehow wending his way up and over the Merrimack River to Canterbury Center and out six miles past farmhouses and beaver ponds to Shaker Village and the little homemade house that Dudley had built. Like many another big city pilgrim to the countryside, Vince was being exposed to a large and unanticipated dose of culture shock. Near the wood stove and beneath shelves full of canning jars, he sat in on a poetry reading

---

63. Peter Colby was an extraordinarily talented person. He made banjos for the Vega Company of Boston and worked in the construction of iron lungs for use by polio victims. While a college student, he built an authentic replica of a flintlock Kentucky rifle and won a shooting competition with it.

and encountered traditional dance tunes for the first time. "I was blown away," he remembers. "It was profoundly simple and beautiful music." At the time, in the city, he was playing electric guitar in both jazz and soul bands in and around Roxbury, walking an interracial walk that most white musicians never navigated beyond the talking stage. Through his jazz training, he had been drawn to the creation of harmony lines, and once he heard Dudley and Joe Ryan launch into the strains of "Petronella," he said to himself: "I can do that!"

Dudley needed a bass player for a gig in New Boston, and Vince O'Donnell agreed to bring along his Gretsch electric guitar and to play bass runs with the group. As it happened, Vince was looking for a way to re-explore his classical violin training, and traditional country dance music presented him with a creative opportunity to do so. "It was an accessible branch of music from a time period that touched me," Vince remembers. "It wasn't classical, but it was rooted in something that goes back to the time when classical music was developing. It struck me as being really accessible, and I was attracted to the idea of musicians who were doing other things in their lives." In short order, he established himself as a mainstay in Dudley's growing country dance band, a group he described as "trusting each other and diving into the music." He became Dudley's close personal friend as well. Vince's electric guitar can be heard in "Dorset Four Hand Reel" on "The Orange Album," in the notes of "Earl of Mansfield" on the *Mistwold* recording, and on the violin on a number of the other tunes from the group's early output.

The idea of "musicians who were doing other things in their lives" covered a broad swath of interests and endeavors during the rural Yankee renaissance of the late 1960s and early 1970s. A number of the Canterbury group were back-to-the-landers; Sylvia Miskoe, Vince, and Dudley were all raising children; Bob McQuillen was a teacher, Pete Colby and Allan Block were craftsmen, and other members were professors or otherwise employed by colleges, universities, or "alternative schools," several of which sprouted up in the Merrimack watershed and in the Monadnock region. Dudley and Vince devoted time and talent to a New Hampshire Free School that taught traditional skills to students through what amounted to apprenticeships. The experience ultimately served as a model for local public schools struggling to provide effective new models for non-traditional learners.

Vince was also in the process of constructing a remarkable career as a leader in the affordable housing movement in Boston and around the country. The racial history and dynamics of Boston presented a major-league-level challenge to anyone with a sense of mission, fairness, and responsibility. Vince helped to lead a cohort of ideals and results-driven reformers who, over several decades, have made a real difference in the prospects for poor people in the old City on a Hill. In his life, the rigors of urban activism mixed with the routine of making the rounds at dances in New Boston, Francestown, Nelson, Fitzwilliam, Harrisville, and Peterborough. Along with the music, Vince and Dudley explored each other's insights about social justice in general and about pacifism in particular, and the two became close friends.[64]

Art Bryan was a Jersey boy who had summered in the Monadnock region before going on to Middlebury College. Around 1964, a college classmate asked Art to play at a wedding in Cambridge, Massachusetts, a place he had never visited. The afternoon before the wedding, Art found himself alone in the city in a strange apartment near the Charles, when the phone rang. The caller was Neil Rossi, and he asked to speak to the apartment's occupant, saying that he was needed to play guitar at a dance. Art was a committed "folkie" himself, and he answered that the tenant of the house was not at home and volunteered the information that he played the guitar. He was promptly given directions to the performance venue, where he soon he found himself tuning up with Dudley Laufman and his friends. The music was captivating, as was a rollicking all-night party afterwards at a Harvard Square commune called Old Joe Clark's, which was interrupted three times by the Cambridge Police. The wedding, next day, played out as an anticlimax; Art had found

---

64. Interview with Vince O'Donnell, 5/18/22.

himself on a path that he would travel for the rest of his life. A few weeks later, back in his dorm at Middlebury, Art took a fateful phone call from Dudley, asking him if he'd take $10 to play at a dance in Acworth, New Hampshire. He was in the band.

Dudley knew that it was not enough to simply allow a young musician to sit in. After young people took the daunting step of sticking their necks out in public performance, they should be made to feel both welcome and accomplished. Youthful newcomers were publicly introduced and thanked, and thus were more likely to practice all the more diligently at home and then to become regulars at the dances. Mentorship was a skill worth reviving; perhaps it was the most crucial component of the performing arts.

Dances were held at points on the Yankee constellation of town houses, dance halls, churches, and college campuses that threaded out across the New England landscape, and at Dudley and Cynthia's handmade homestead on Shaker Road. The common denominator was the spontaneous delight engendered by the music. Dudley once said that "many of us Yankee musicians, callers, and dancers might show subtle body language and joy in response to the musical occasion, but when it comes to facial expression, with Sylvia Miskoe, the music just makes her beam with happiness."[65] Some nights were transcendent and some were just hilarious, such as the time at a dance when Nick Howe's big tethered dog pulled Bob McQuillen's piano right across the floor in the middle of a performance of "Chorus Jig."

Marilyn Patterson attended a "Dudley Dance" in the fall of 1971 in New Boston, New Hampshire, and wrote feelingly about her experience: "There's a kind of mystique afoot about square dancing that can make the saddest person laugh, the loneliest person alone no more, the shiest of us free and outgoing…There was among the Friday night dancers a split evident even to a child's eye. There were the devoted Dudley followers, the folks who will come from the farthest reaches…to attend his dances. They were the ones who knew the calls practically before he gave them and could execute them with

---

65. Quoted in 2011 N.H. Governor's Arts Awards entry.

precision. Then there were the ones among us who hadn't danced since the fifth-grade gym class days. We were the ones who looked confused no matter what he said and whose execution was faulty at best. But no matter how much you stumbled, the lilting music went on. If you were lucky, one of the experts was nearby and would shout an instruction in your ear or point you in the proper direction. If you weren't lucky, you just continued to stumble to the end and enjoyed the fact that everyone else was stumbling with you…It was your dance to share…If you missed the first New Boston dance, fear not, it was only one of three. The next is to be November 12…if you came and spent the evening bewildered, again, fear not. For us it was the second Dudley dance, and we were bewildered only half the time. There's progress to be made in November."[66]

Dudley's constant appearances throughout the New England countryside were building a strong momentum that would define contradance across the continent and, ultimately, over a half-century and still counting. A growing number of musicians would arrive at the same conclusion that Art Bryan came to the first time he parked his car at the Nelson Town Hall, stepped out into the evening air, and heard the sound of veteran local contradance musicians in full swing. A voice inside him said, firmly and swiftly: "*This* is what I want to do."[67]

---

66. Marilyn Patterson, "For Rollicking Fun, Try A Square Dance," *The Goffstown News*, October 14, 1971.

67. Interview with Art Bryan, 5/22.

$$\Longrightarrow 9 \Longleftarrow$$

Rum and Onions in the Folk Revival

THE EARLY 1960s saw the beginnings of a period that would become known as the folk music revival in Boston and Cambridge.[68] In 1959, a Boston University drop-out named Joan Baez had been too nervous to perform in a tiny Harvard Square room without the reassuring presence of her parents. About a year later, she recorded and released a record album that sold half a million copies, then in 1962 her portrait graced the cover of *Time* magazine. Although she was the most famous of the Boston-Cambridge folk singers, her work was only a part of a broad renaissance in traditional song that saw the seats of more than three dozen coffeehouses fill to capacity in Boston and elsewhere in New England seven nights a week. Huge crowds gathered at folk festivals held at Newport, in Philadelphia, and in upstate New York. For the most part, this explosion of acoustic music focused on ballads and blues performed by singers wielding six-string Gibsons or Martins; in the mainstream of the folk revival, for the most part, people were either playing guitar or listening to someone who was.

Square and contradancers and their exotic array of instruments mingled among the new-coming crowds of the folk revival like a

---

68. Thomas S. Curren, *I Believe I'll Go Back Home*, (Boston, Amherst; Bright Leaf Press, 2021).

bearded group of Jewish scholars at a staid ecumenical breakfast. When it came to take the full measure of the urban folk revival, it was clear that the country dancers had gotten there first. The strathspeys, contras, and jigs of dance traditions were far older than the "swing that hammer" and "let me be your salty dog" style of songs that were becoming the coin of the folk revival realm. The rising tide of modern folk music raised all sorts of musical boats and brought the largest generation of young people in American history into an appreciation of the country's diverse and vibrant musical traditions. A number of these became competent musicians in a variety of realms and styles, but it was clear that the Yankee instrumentalists who had been playing traditional dance music for decades were well ahead of the game.

Much as in the case of bluegrass music, contradance playing was often a matter of gathering good musicians together based on their availability for a certain gig. It was usually the dance caller who put together the playing roster, and Dudley Laufman had a rich list of instrumentalists that he could call upon. He booked an ambitious schedule of dances in East Concord, Nelson, Tamworth, and at other points of the compass at town halls, church basements, and college campuses throughout New England. Dudley recalls one of the more eventful gigs: "In the fall of 1964, Joe Ryan, Dave Fuller, Jack Sloanaker and myself provided music for dancing and intermission entertainment during the Vermont Old Time Fiddlers Contest at Goddard College. As we were getting ready to leave on Sunday night, a chap who introduced himself as Ralph Rinzler said he was a 'scout' for the Newport Folk Festival, and he would like to arrange for the four of us to come to Newport the following summer to conduct workshops on New England dance music. The ensuing months saw a lot of phone conversations and letters back and forth between Ralph and me. I tried to tell him that we should bring along Newt Tolman, our flute player from Nelson. Ralph had never heard of a flute being used with fiddles. In fact, he had a hard time believing that there was any traditional music at all in New England."

The idea that "real traditional American music" was assumed to be an exclusive product of southern Appalachia, the Mississippi delta, and the western prairies had become dogma among the urban folk crowd. The fact that something had evolved in Manhattan that could be called "big-time folk music" seemed more than a bit ironic. Ralph Rinzler was, without question, among the most capable and, in the long run, most accomplished of the leaders in the new endeavor.[69] The encounter in the parking lot at Goddard College set a series of events in motion that would transform Dudley Laufman's life in music.

In February of 1965, the musicians from the Goddard gig (with the addition of Newt Tolman and bass player Jack O'Connor) played the first of what would be many engagements at the Club 47, a folk music coffeehouse located near Harvard Square. At an earlier location at 47 Mount Auburn Street, the club had acted as the artistic incubator for Joan Baez, the Charles River Valley Boys, Tom Rush, Jackie Washington,[70] Eric von Schmidt, Dayle Stanley, and the Jim Kweskin Jug Band, and as the New England port of call for traditional American folk artists from throughout the country such as Doc Watson, Mississippi John Hurt, Almeda Riddle, and Hobart Smith.

Newt Tolman took it upon himself to scout out the Club 47 on his own terms. "When I arrived, a tall young man wearing a faded blue shirt and dungarees was sweeping the floor. I thought he was the janitor, and he was—and also the proprietor. A pleasant, rather sleepy-looking fellow, by name Jim Rooney, he is a left-handed guitar player and sings ballads with considerable ability." The two men hit it off. After sizing up young Jim Rooney and deciding that he liked the cut of his jib, Newt went over the roster of the New Hampshire contradance musicians, which included: "a pianist who is a children's psychiatrist at Harvard. Accordionist, former fighter pilot turned

---

69. Rinzler's prominent role in the festival and at the Center for Folklife Programs led the Smithsonian Institution to name the Ralph Rinzler Folklife Archives and Collections in his honor in 1998.

70. Jack Landron was Jackie's given name. He and Joe Val (Joseph Valiente) of Everett were among the folk revival artists born in the Boston area.

carpenter. First fiddle, a teacher who went native and started an arts-and-crafts business up in the mountains some place. Second fiddle a young professor of philosophy in one of our ex-dairy farm colleges. Bass player, an engineer or something, in electronics. Organizer and master of ceremonies of the group is Dudley Laufman, our popular local square dance caller...a latter day pioneer who lives with his wife and several kids in a remarkable igloo fashioned out of odds and ends, up in the old Shaker Village of Canterbury."[71]

In the order of that presentation, he seems to have described Jack Sloanaker, Dave Fuller, Joe Ryan, Nicholas Howe, Jack O'Connor, and Dudley Laufman. Tolman could have described himself as the descendant of a Revolutionary War veteran who lived in a rambling old family farmhouse on several hundred acres, owned a Rolls-Royce as well as a tractor, and was married to a licensed New Hampshire hunting guide. Newt had been playing classical flute since the days when, as a boy, he had performed for an elderly John Phillip Sousa. He once claimed, with characteristic authority, that he was capable of playing "The Stars and Stripes Forever" on a limp dandelion stem.[72]

This was the ensemble that would take the stage at 47 Palmer Street in Cambridge. Dudley's written instructions to the group had been succinct: "All jigs and reels played thru four times unless otherwise. Dress: informal. No dungarees, plaid shirts, string ties. Not too folksy or woodsy...Be careful of and make allowances for traffic in Boston and Cambridge..." The program that they presented in the city venue took advantage of a higher degree of artistic license than might have been the case in the Nelson Town Hall; in addition to tunes like "Forester's Hornpipe," "Chorus Jig," and "Smash The Window," Dudley read a few of his poems, Joe Ryan played the musical saw and sang a sea chanty, and then he joined in with Dudley and Jack to sing "Marie's Wedding." Newt added a few selections of his own, choosing two Irish jigs, "Swimming in the

---

71. Newt Tolman, *Berkshire Eagle*, May 13, 1966, 2. Used by permission.
72. When he was asked about his schedule, Newt once declared that he began writing "about an hour before I wake up in the morning."

Gutter," and "Rum and Onions" that, as he put it, had "probably not been heard in Cambridge for a century or more, if ever—and not things the average folk musician could learn in a hurry." As Newt remembered it, "the applause was definitely louder each time we did an instrumental number…It was great fun while it lasted."[73]

Five months later, the troupe, augmented by about a dozen New Hampshire dancers and a total of ten musicians, made the trek to Freebody Park, the site of the Newport Folk Festival. On July 25, 1965, they were scheduled to play at the afternoon "workshop" session before later opening the evening concert. The dancers were just setting up on a low stage in front of a modest but enthusiastic audience when a huge crowd of people swarmed down from a nearby hill and began roiling aimlessly around. Dudley decided to jettison the carefully planned workshop,[74] as he said "contra dances fell off the program and the whole thing turned into a rip roaring old time square dance." The impromptu multitude, they later learned, was the crowd that spilled out of an abbreviated set by Bob Dylan with the Paul Butterfield Blues Band, a three-tune run-through that would eventually take on mythic proportions.

Dudley continues the account: "That evening we opened the concert. Loring Puffer nearly threw up when we mounted the stage and faced 16,000 people. I asked Harvey Tolman to play a little of 'Money Musk' as a strathspey before we danced it as a reel. He borrowed Jack O'Connor's fiddle, found it not tuned to his liking, and said 'Shit' over the mic. But we got going and what fun we had on that stage to that great music. When we exited after thunderous ovation, we were greeted by Pete Seeger and Theo Bikel who both said we sounded like a Handel concerto. Took a long time to come down

---

73. Dudley and his group played the Club 47 on seven occasions, including a children's program on 2/27/65, "Robert Burns Nights" in 1966 and 1967, and a "Sugaring Off" party in the spring of 1966.

74. His planned workshop presentation had included a dozen contras, hornpipes, and reels, everything from "Haste to the Wedding" to "Hinky-Dinky Parlez-Vous."

from all that heady experience." Tunes played and danced in the evening concert included "Sherbrooke Slide," "Petronella," "Ross's Reel," and "Money Musk," all of them played in a stirring tempo that had many in the audience, including Joan Baez, up and on their feet and dancing in the aisles. This was a folk revival performance at its very best: traditional music, able musicians, and an enthusiastic and participatory audience.

After the heady experience of Newport, the members of the orchestra settled into their accustomed rounds of dances in local halls and hinterland concerts. The six-person group appeared again at the Club 47 in October, January, and March. That summer, Dudley and fiddler Doug Cox drove out to a gig in Alexandria, Ohio. On the way back, they decided to swing over to Petersburg, New York, west of Bennington, to scout out the Beers family estate, site of the upcoming 1966 Fox Hollow Folk Festival. The grounds where the gathering was to be held included a natural amphitheater that had sprouted up to a growth of young woods, trees about four inches through at the butt. Two men, stripped to the waist and sweating, were struggling to saw a few of them down by hand when Laufman and Cox drove up. It turned out that the amateur sawyers were Fiddler Beers and Boston folk radio personality Robert J. Lurtsema, whose girths easily exceeded the breadth of their experience as a woodsman. Cox proceeded to shimmy up one of the trees and bent it down towards the ground like a swung birch, whereupon Dudley sliced through the straining trunk fibers with a sharp axe, chopping the tree down with a couple of deft strokes. In little time, they had three trees on the ground. Beers and Lurtsema seemed unamused, so the New Hampshire men took their leave.

Dudley and the musicians that he had traveled with to Newport were invited to perform at the 1967 and 1968 Fox Hollow Festivals, sharing the stage with dulcimer player Jean Ritchie, the wonderful musical group called The Golden Ring, and storyteller Marshall Dodge, among many others. Dudley established the rules for the Canterbury Orchestra: "No leads, no medleys, and I'm in charge." In *Sing Out!* magazine, columnist Israel Young wrote enthusiastically about the performance of the New Hampshire musicians, which included newcomer Ted Levin on piano. At Fox Hollow, the group caught the attention of Sandy and Carolyn Paton, the owners of Folk-Legacy Records of Huntington, Vermont, who approached Dudley about the idea of making a record with their company. Word came that Joan Baez had made her way to the Nelson Town Hall, where she was seen dancing with Frankie Upton. The tempo seemed to be picking up a bit in the old country of contradance.

Magic at the Middlesex School and Beyond

IN JULY OF 1965, the Newport Folk Festival had seen Dudley's musicians billed as The New England Contra Dance Group. In January of 1966, they were listed in the Club 47 as Dudley Laufman and Friends. Ten months later, at a December 9 appearance, they were billed as Dudley Laufman and the Canterbury Country Orchestra. The name change had come only after some considerable discussion. Dudley originally had wanted to call the group The Nelson Country Dance Orchestra, but Newt Tolman thought that the Canterbury title would be more appropriate. When Dudley pointed out that he was the only member who lived in Canterbury, Newt asked rhetorically how many members of the Budapest String Quartet hailed from Budapest. The answer was: one. Canterbury Country Dance Orchestra it was.

The components of Dudley's unique style are worth considering, partly because they are so idiosyncratic and partly because they became so influential. As Dudley put it: "Most of what we play is traditional dance music that originated in the British Isles and was composed by wandering pipers, fiddlers, and dancing masters mostly nameless to us now."[75] By the late 1960s, Dudley had spent

---

75. Liner notes to the 2000 CD release of the collection called *Canterbury Country Dance Orchestra with Dudley Laufman*.

about fifteen years developing the concept of a distinctive "sound" to apply to that repertoire of ancient tunes, one through which he could define his personal stamp on the music. His earliest influences would have been the Quimby's repertoire that he first heard at Mistwold Farm, followed thereafter by tunes he learned from Maude Ashman, Lin Cady, Ralph Page and the Nelson crew, and then from Arthur Hanson. His basic ideal had been formed by the band that Ralph Page assembled at Bell's Studio in Peterborough: the piano, two fiddles, bass, and accordion ensemble that had played masterfully behind Page's singing calls. Dudley had been deeply moved by a 1957 record album of jigs and reels created by classically trained Irish musician David Curry and his orchestra.[76] Curry's group had a rich and imposing sound that combined a strong piano base and climbing string arpeggios. The resulting musical presentation felt both stately and fluid, a key addition to Dudley's internal "ear."

Some consideration might be given to what could be seen as a Quaker influence in Dudley's music. This perspective might be dynamic in philosophical terms as much as in musical ones. Quakers valued, among other things, the practice of silent reflection that could draw forth the essence of the soul. Perhaps this was what Dudley had in mind when he encouraged spontaneous creativity in the musicians he convened, and perhaps this was also what he was driving at when he said that "joy comes as the dancer stops dancing to the calls and starts dancing to the music." The presence of an inner light could be applied to music as well as to meditative prayer.

He brought a strong sense of mission to his calling as a dance master. A good part of this dynamic played out in the service of tradition. Dudley and his colleagues treated the old tunes and dance steps as if they were illuminated manuscripts that might otherwise have likely fallen into the hands of the heathen or the heedless. He has been quick to turn any journey into a pilgrimage and to treat the old landscapes, the old halls, and the resting places of musicians past

---

76. *My Ireland,* David Curry Orchestra, Capital Records DT 10028, featured a
    cover photograph of an ancient Irish woman playing the harp.

as shrines. Musical remembrance can transcend time and serve to emancipate our better natures along with our memories. It may well be that the act of listening to an old tune like "Childgrove" can give our hearts as deep a sense of English history as devoting a week to memorizing the genealogies of the Plantagenets or the Tudors.

Yet there is a dynamic to the presiding role of dance master that might not pass muster at a leaderless Quaker meeting. Magic is afoot in music, and it often takes a priestess or a priest to convene the hall, wielding a concertina or a fiddle that wafts forth tunes as if they were clouds of incense. The old callers seemed to have been quick to develop an identity for their dances based upon the stamp of personality and practice, and it wasn't long before the term "Dudley Dance" entered the lexicon of country dancers throughout the region.

As the 1970s began, Dudley was working with some of the best musicians in New England. Scattered over the countryside, most of them were not well known, but individually they were first-rate, and collectively they constituted an extraordinarily talented fellowship. The idea of making a record on Folk-Legacy Records seemed like a natural, since from its inception in 1961 the Vermont-based label had focused on recording outstanding traditional musicians. Both Sandy and Caroline Paton were enthusiastic about the Canterbury group, but progress hit a snag when Sandy fell and broke his leg, delaying action on the project. After some thought, Newt Tolman decided that he was disinclined to make an appearance on a recording. This became a deal-killer for Paton, who had, quite understandably, focused much of his attention on Newt's unique abilities. Yet talented flautist Larry Delorier had found his way over from New England College in Henniker and soon ably occupied the woodwind seat in the group. As fiddler Nicholas S. Howe told Dudley at the time, the work that the Canterbury musicians was doing was "probably as close to the eighteenth century as anything left in the New World." It was time to make a record.[77]

---

77. Nicholas S. Howe in a letter to Dudley Laufman, 1971.

Jack Sloanaker had created an F&W Records label, and on it he had produced two 33⅓ LP albums by the youthful players of the Farm and Wilderness String Band. Dudley approached Jack straight on: could the Canterbury group put out a record of their own on the F&W label? Jack answered in the affirmative, and plans began for a recording session to be held at the chapel of the Middlesex School on Lowell Road in Concord, Massachusetts. The graceful, dignified building had been erected in 1924 in honor of graduates of the school who had died in World War I. The acoustics in the chapel were superb; Jack had become familiar with them while he was a Middlesex faculty member, and he knew that the Telemann Society had recorded classical music pieces in the building. Jack and Seth Gibson of the school began arrangements, and the Middlesex administration agreed to exchange single-day use of the facility in return for a special concert to be held for students on the afternoon following the taping session. The recording date was set for Saturday, September 25, 1971.

A bit later on, Newt Tolman would observe that Dudley made as much mention in his album liner notes of the roughly dozen Canterbury-associated musicians who *didn't* appear on the record as the ones who *did*, but the ten who convened in the carpeted chapel in their stockinged feet made history on that warm fall day out on the old road between Concord and Carlisle.[78] Bob McQuillen, who once described himself as "an old-time dance piano player," laid down the keyboard foundation for the group that included Jack Sloanaker on bass; Dave Fuller, accordion; Larry Delorier, flute, piccolo, and penny-whistle; Jerry Weene on fiddle and mandolin; Peter Colby playing banjo and autoharp; Ted Levin, Nicholas S. Howe, and

---

78. Other CCDO musicians mentioned in the album notes included Newt Tolman, flute; Jack O'Connor, fiddle, bass, accordion, banjo; Joe Ryan, fiddle; Walter Lob, fiddle; Gene Morrow, oboe; Sylvia Sawyer Miskoe, accordion; Don Braley, fiddle; Omer Marcoux, fiddle; Mark Hanson, guitar, and David Raitt, bass. Vince O'Donnell was also well established in the band by this time, but the birth of his first child took precedence over the recording date for "The Blue Album."

Allan Block on fiddles; and Dudley Laufman playing accordion and leading the session. Seth Gibson handled the recording of the sixteen tunes that Jack Sloanaker used to produce the fourteen-cut LP called the *Canterbury Country Dance Orchestra*[79] that later became known as "The Blue Album." There was no run-through or warm-up, other than at a dance a bit earlier in the month up in Acworth. Coffee, inspiration, and the accumulated ebb-and-flow of about a decade of dance-floor experience constituted the sum of the preparation that the gathered musicians drew upon.

"Irish-American Reel" was the first song that the group launched into, finished in a single take of three minutes and thirty-three seconds. Seth Gibson re-wound the tape and played it back to test out volume, balance, and tone. Listening to the replay, Dudley Laufman broke into tears. It was more than a keeper; it was a classic, and everyone in the old chapel knew that in an instant. Such things don't happen often, and when they do, you learn to just hitch up your britches, carpe the old diem, and keep on playing.

The raw tapes were set down on twelve-inch reels which were taken up and the business of production of the *Canterbury Country Dance Orchestra* began, a complex process which would involve months of work on Jack Sloanaker's part before the album was actually released the following spring. What ensued was not just a wonderful record album, it was a talisman crafted magically out of time, heritage, and place. The record became a soundtrack fit to play while stuffing a holiday turkey, while splitting a pile of firewood, and, once cassettes were invented, when attempting to transform a tedious drive on Routes 90, 91, 93, or 95 into a pilgrimage. Young back-to-the-land women in New Hampshire asked to have "The Blue Album" cued up on the turntable as they navigated through the long voyage of a home birth, and their babies grew up listening to the well-worn recorded strains of its piano, flutes, banjo, bass, accordion, and fiddles. Jack Sloanaker referred to the recording as

---

79. *Canterbury Country Dance Orchestra*, LP, F&W Records FW-3, recorded 1971, released 1972.

an example of artistic "spontaneous combustion." In his newsletter, Ralph Page rated it "highly recommended" and said that he "hope they sell a million LP's."

Half a century later, the opening notes of "Farewell to Whiskey" still serve to ignite time and space, accelerating on grasshopper wings into "Money Musk" and soaring up in flight to the cruising altitude of the transcendent "Petronella." For the majority of listeners, the tunes take them where they will in thought and emotion through the magic that only music can conjure up. Those who wanted to delve into the actual provenances of the pieces could find connection to musical ancestries that sprang from Irish, Balkan, Dutch, Scottish, and English traditions. Through these tunes, listeners could make acquaintance with a handsome Dutch prince, a beguiling Italian dancer, a sturdy set of English stag hunters, and a fetching Scottish lass. One could appreciate the good taste demonstrated by Ludwig von Beethoven when he purloined "Yarmouth Reel" and inserted the tune into his published "Twelve Contratanzes." He was not the only borrower of the old airs; as Nick Howe noted, Handel had regularly "lifted thematic material that he would have heard at any crossroad in England." Dudley and his crew were fetching these ingredients home from antiquity and setting them up on the Yankee cupboard shelf where they could be readily sprinkled into a stew or a chowder or whatever else was percolating on the homestead wood stove or flowing from the cider press out in the shed.

As had been agreed upon, after a wonderful lunch Dudley and the musicians put on a *tour de force* concert for an audience of Middlesex School students and faculty who quickly filled the chapel pews. The gathering took the form of a combined lecture and performance of tunes, a few of which repeated the recorded work of the morning while the remainder sprang from whole other worlds of source, whimsey, and tradition. Dudley took the podium as a sort of guest lecturer, presenting an engaging definition of a jig, which the group then illustrated in the tune "Smash The Windows;" then a reel, "Peter Street;" a hornpipe, with "Fisher's Hornpipe;" and another dance tune, the rollicking "Huntsman's Chorus," which had been set down earlier in the day. Allan Block sang the old Ozark folk fiddle tune "The Arkansas Traveler," and then went on to play a ragtime number called "The Hesitation Blues." Dudley then introduced the members of the group, cued up "Glise à Sherbrooke," and followed by describing the topic of Baltic tunes such as "Kalendera Kolo" from the morning's recording session. He then gave an overview of contradance steps in the calls to "Petronella," giving the students a sample of dance calling in action.

Peter Colby described his handmade autoharp to the audience and played a sparkling version of a ragtime piano tune titled "Darktown Dandies." The group followed with "Yarmouth Reel" and "The Wind That Shakes The Barley." The concert moved towards conclusion with a couple of rowdy English drinking songs led by Dudley: "Hal and Tow," out of Cornwall back in the 1600s, and "Who's The Fool, Now?" from London around the same time.[80] The concert ended with a stirring version of "Prince William" by the whole group, playing, singing in unison, and marching together out of the hall in time to the music, accompanied by the audience's enthusiastic applause. A magical session of music-making came to an end as the early New England Indian summer moved one day closer to the falling leaves of autumn.

The new year of 1972 would prove to be among the most active in the life of the group. On January 7, the Canterbury musicians arrived at the Quincy House Dining Room at Harvard University that kicked off a five-month series of weekly dances that stretched through the end of May. For some time, conventional square dances had been part of the scene at both Harvard and MIT, and the arrival of the Canterbury outfit was a memorable event.

---

80. The singing of "Hal and Tow" is still a highlight of May Day in Helston. "Who's The Fool Now" was set in writing by Thomas Ravenscroft about the year 1609. As sung by Maddy Prior, this old tune has been a standard in the playlist of the English group Steeleye Span.

On Sunday, May 28, 1972, an "Old Fashioned Folk Concert" was held at the Fitzwilliam Ski Area located between Winchendon, Massachusetts, and Keene, New Hampshire. Featured on the bill were Dudley and members of the Canterbury Country Dance Orchestra: Bob McQuillen, Dave Fuller, Ted Levin, Larry Delorier, Pete Colby, and Jack Sloanaker, among others. In sets played over the course of a long spring day, forty tunes were performed by the group, augmented by musicians Newt Tolman and Kay Gilbert, Randy Miller, and Rodney Miller. Solos were played by Dudley Laufman, Peter Colby, Newt Tolman, Ted Levin, and Ken Siegal. A rousing version of "Devil's Dream" was contributed by Bob McQuillen, who played an old fiddle and, by way of introduction, told a story about the instrument that dated back to the Civil War and the naval battle at Hampton Roads, Virginia, between the *Monitor* and the *Merrimack*.

On August 1 through 4, 1972, the National Folk Festival was held at Wolf Trap National Park in Vienna, Virginia. Dudley, April Limber, Peter Colby, Bob McQuillen, Art Bryan, Deanna Stiles, and Sandy Campbell made the trip south for the festival, with Dudley in one vehicle and the remainder in Bob McQuillen's smoke-filled Suburban. Art Bryan remembers that after making a late afternoon arrival in Virginia, the group was put up in a local college dorm and then ushered into a lively party that mixed the dynamics of a huge jam session with those of an all-night bender. When they took the stage the next morning in front of more than a thousand dancers and a phalanx of PBS recording cameras, the bleary-eyed contradance group was far from being in fighting trim.

A group of Native American performers sized up the situation and came to the rescue, approaching the stage where the hung-over New Hampshire crew was setting up and passing them styrofoam cups brimming over with beer. Within five minutes or so the Canterbury musicians had gotten the wind back in their sails. They hit overdrive after playing "Chorus Jig," and "Prince William," then scores of dancers began whirling and turning in time to a spirited rendition of "Gaspe Reel." The resulting film documented the music and the dancing and captured the joy that the members of the group took in the experience. The Canterbury Country Dance Orchestra was making some of the best traditional music in the country; they all knew it, and they all reveled in it. Some time later, Art Bryan was shocked when someone yelled to him, "Hey, Art, you're on TV!" and he got to see the PBS broadcast.[81]

Plans were soon underway for a project that would require a good deal of organization on the part of all concerned: the recording of a joint album that came to be titled *The Canterbury Country Orchestra Meets the F&W String Band*.[82] The successful completion of "The Blue Album" raised the idea of a combined record, which eventually was planned to feature eight numbers performed by the conjoined outfits, along with several tunes to be recorded at a later date solely by Dudley's Canterbury group. In the New Year, they had added new recording members Vince O'Donnell on electric guitar and fiddle, Charlene Fagelman on flute, Art Bryan on banjo, and fiddlers Fred Breunig and Jack Perron. The session on August 12, 1972, involved sixty musicians traveling in from all points in the compass, carrying eighteen fiddles, sixteen flutes, five accordions, two basses, nine guitars, piano, piccolo, cello, harmonica, banjo, washboard, and drum board. Final choices were made for inclusion in what came to be known as "The Orange Album."

On August 19, a week after those sessions, Dudley and his group played at an 8 p.m. dance in Somerville. On August 27 they were at the Girl Scout House on Walden Street in Concord, Massachusetts, playing 3–7 p.m, then from 8 p.m. until midnight once in September and October, twice in November, and finishing the year in December.

On the morning of September 23, 1972, the Canterbury Country Dance Orchestra convened again at the Middlesex School Chapel to record the balance of their cuts for inclusion in *The*

---

81. *National Folk Festival in Performance At Wolf Trap* broadcast on PBS 1/6/75.
82. *The Canterbury Country Orchestra Meets the F&W String Band*, F&W Records #4.

Canterbury Country Orchestra Meets The F&W album: "Saddle the Pony," "Miss Dolland's Delight," "Dorset Four-Hand Reel," "Larry O'Gaff," "Balkan Hills Schottische," "Meeting of the Waters," and "Gentle Maiden." This last was a beautiful Irish tune that provided the opportunity for flautists Charlene Fagelman and Larry Delorier to join forces with Art Bryan on guitar and Dudley Laufman on accordion. Later in the day, the group presented a second "tutorial concert" for staff and students at the Middlesex School Chapel, performing eleven tunes with introductory remarks. The group later seems to have recorded additional tunes, some of which may have been included on the *Mistwold* album, and others that eventually were stored away for decades by Jack Sloanaker in reels labeled "Mistwold Outtakes."

On October 8, 1972, a group of players convened again at 11 Miller Street, off Mystic Avenue in Somerville that included Dudley Laufman, accordion and calls; Fred Breunig, fiddle; Susan Champaney, harmonica; Jodi Evans, recorder; Charlene Fagelman, flute; David Langstaff, guitar and recorder; Randy Miller, guitar; Frank Perron, guitar; Jack Perron, fiddle; and Ken Siegal, fiddle. The occasion was a contradance held in the upper floors of a warehouse complex next to the Boston and Maine railroad tracks that housed several apartments and had been the site of the Miller Brothers Coffin Factory since 1880s. Jack Sloanaker was in attendance, and concentrated on recording the musicians rather than on playing. The twelve tunes totaled about sixty-nine minutes of music, calls, and dancing with a sound that hearkened back to the days before keyboards and basses. Dudley's calls ride up and over the music, and the tape includes the dynamic sound of dozens of dancers pounding away, bare feet slapping on the floor of the old factory. The remarkable reel-to-reel recording of *Live at The Coffin Factory* was cleaned, restored, and digitized in 2017.[83]

---

83. Despite the inexorable forces of urban renewal, the old building at 11 Miller Street is still intact, serving now as studio space for a wide variety of artists.

That month of November was a representative snapshot of the life of Dudley and the musicians he played with. On the first day of the month, the group gave two concerts at the Roundhill Community Center in Greenwich, Connecticut. Next day they played an afternoon concert at Hendrie Hall on the Yale campus at New Haven, then scooted up the Connecticut River Valley along the course of Interstate 91 to a dance that night at the Chelsea House Cafe in West Brattleboro, Vermont. On the 4th, it was back down to the Southern Connecticut College in New Haven; the 5th was an evening dance at Strafford, Vermont; the 6th saw the group playing at a dance in the Durham, New Hampshire Grange Hall, and on the 7th at the Unitarian Church in Carlisle, Massachusetts. On November 9, Dudley gave a daytime poetry reading at the Unitarian Church in Manchester, New Hampshire, followed that evening by a dance back down Interstate 93 at the Cambridge Friends School. On the 10th, the group was at the Unitarian Church in Manchester again, on the 14th in South Amherst, Massachusetts. On the 20th, the group convened again at the Grange Hall in Durham; on the 21st at Pat's Peak Ski Area in Henniker, NH, the next night at the Chelsea House in Brattleboro, the 28th at Hancock Town Hall, the 29th at the Tamworth Town Hall, and then they finished the month in a performance on the 30th at the Peabody-Essex Museum in the old spice port of Salem, Massachusetts.

In the midst of touring and performing across the New England countryside, the roster of Canterbury musicians convened again at the Middlesex School Chapel November 18, 1972, for sessions that were included in their second recording, the *Mistwold*[84] album. In addition to the fifteen cuts chosen for inclusion on the LP, a total of more than thirty outtakes and alternate numbers were set on tape in this and in the previous sessions. The tunes not chosen for release included outstanding renditions of the "Ash Grove," "The German

---

84. *Mistwold*, Canterbury Country Dance Orchestra, F&W Records FW 5, 1974.

Beau," "Pipe On The Hob," "DeMartelly," and "Finnegan's Wake." Nearly fifty years later, when first heard after digitization in 2017, they sounded as clean and tight as anything the group ever recorded.

Mistwold is a tour de force. Distinct in character from "The Blue Album," it largely meets the standard of excellence set by that earlier release. Noteworthy cuts include Dudley's compositions of "Mistwold" and "Glenn Towle," a stirring medley on autoharp and harmonica by Peter Colby, and "Madame Bonaparte," a beautiful piece written in Killarney in the 1790s. The tune begins quietly with Larry Delorier's flute solo and Art Bryan's guitar, then Dave Fuller's accordion and the fiddles come in, Bob McQuillen's deep piano notes plod along as majestically as a Clydesdale, and the entire group soars towards a crescendo of precision and abandon that is as climactic as a hearing of Pachelbel's Canon. Several times in the course of four-and-a-half-minutes of music, when a steam heat valve hisses loudly in the building, it comes in right *exactly* on the beat.[85]

Dudley wrote about the session: "At nine in the morning we one-and-two into the chapel. It is all marble and chandeliers and smells like a church. Dave is trying out a new tune and Bob is learning the chords on the piano. The sound echoes like bells. Seth Gibson is setting up the tape recorder, and tells us that there is coffee and donuts over in his house if we want. I put my stuff in one of the private pews and slam the gate like a player leaving the penalty box and skate over to Seth's for a cup. Soon we all arrive, get tuned, make some test runs for positions, take off our shoes, lock the doors, signal for silence…'Mistwold, take 1.' Then listen to the playback…a half minute of silver hissing room sound, then music like crystal. At noon we all flock over to the dining hall where we are treated to a roast beef dinner with all the fixings. Then a beer and a short nap, and back to the recording. Late afternoon, when we are all done, gather in Seth's living room for a beer and a complete playback. Dark outside…"

---

85. A hornpipe, originating in Ireland at a time when Irish sentiment ran high for the Catholic French.

The *Mistwold* album remains today as a reminder of the wonderful year of 1972. It is still as fresh today as it was on the day it was recorded with the characteristic, classic Canterbury Country Dance Orchestra sound that owed much to the Middlesex Chapel. After the musicians finished these sessions, they were not to return to that unique venue for about a dozen years. Yet the combination of three formally released albums, two student concerts, and at least two other recording sessions over the course of only three years constitutes a body of creativity that any musicians would have been proud to claim as their life's work. As Dudley suggested at the time: "So, put on the record, have a good drink in hand, and sit back and fantasize. That's what I do."[86]

It seems fitting to close this chapter with the thoughts of two of the senior players in the Canterbury Country Dance Orchestra, written in letters that were sent to Dudley after the release of the first copies of "The Blue Album," in March of 1972. The first of these was a note of congratulations from Newt Tolman:

> *It's a hell of a fine accomplishment on the part of yourself, Jack Sloanaker, and all hands!…The overall performance sounds unbelievably smooth and well-coordinated; the average educated listener would simply not imagine that the group had not rehearsed the program over a very considerable time…Tempo is excellent throughout, and this makes the recording unique for dancing purposes…this one is in a class by itself…Nothing remotely like it has been done before as far as I know…the Canterbury record is more than a milestone in recorded music. We now have an orchestral recording containing some of our "Nelson"*

---

86. Laufman, *Mistwold*, op. cit.

> *music which we can enjoy ourselves, and be proud to*
> *play in the months and years to come.*
>
>   *Best, Newt*

The letter speaks for itself, yet a few things seem worth noting. Newton Tolman was a taciturn Yankee whose ancestral tenure in the shadow of Mount Monadnock went back to the time before America existed as a nation. As much as he took to Dudley Laufman, and as much as he enjoyed throwing his performing lot in with Sloanaker, Levin, O'Donnell, Colby, McQuillen, Howe, et al., he had chosen to refrain from calling the band "The Nelson Country Dance Orchestra" as Dudley had initially suggested. Yet, with the evidence of "The Blue Record" in hand, he dismissed the constitutional reservations of a gentleman of the old school and jettisoned personal pride as well. Newt Tolman is *all in* here, and he's throwing the totality of his family's local heritage in play as well, referring to the recording as "our Nelson music." It would be difficult to imagine a more powerful and considered endorsement from this man.

Bob McQuillen was cut from a completely different bolt of personality fabric than Newt Tolman. Yet he, too, is placing all his chips on this recording. For a man of Bob's stature and talents to refer to this session as a high point in his life is enormously significant. His service in the military, his decades of devotion to public education, his years of playing with Ralph Page and a host of other fine musicians, and his role as the composer of thousands of memorable tunes are all accomplishments that he chose to rank with the joint venture that was The Canterbury Country Dance Orchestra. This was praise of the finest kind, coupled with affection expressed out of the soul of a big man who harbored deep emotions:

> *The beautiful record arrived Wed. and we listen*
> *to nothing else!...I really wanted to tell you how*
> *overjoyed I am to have been a part of making that*
> *music with you all and to thank you for including me*

in your group. It was truly a high point in my life— such fun to do that day and to listen to now. I thank you, Dudley Laufman, for many joys.

Sincerely and from a loving heart,
Bob McQuillen.[87]

87. Personal notes from Newt Tolman and from Bob McQuillen to Dudley Laufman, early 1972.

March 11, 1965

Mr. Dudley Laufman
Shaker Road
Canterbury, New Hampshire

Dear Dudley:

Many thanks for your note. We are still interested in having you come to
Newport. I cannot at the moment be certain on what specific dates we would
want you to perform. We would want a small group of musicians and a caller
and a group of dancers. Hopefully, the caller could teach dances to a group
of people who would attend a workshop on New England Country Dance. I do
hope you can bring Newt Tollman, who would also hopefully participate in a
workshop on wind instruments in folk music.

Let me know what you would consider an ideal and representative group of
musicians. Musicians are paid at the rate of $50.00 per performing day.
We could not pay dancers at the same rate, obviously.

Let me hear from you further.

Best regards,

Ralph Rinzler

RR:mv

Ralph Rinzler to Dudley Laufman, March 1965 engagement letter for
Newport Folk Festival

Dudley Laufman, unidentified fiddler, Dick Richardson, and "Junior" Richardson at the Laufman home, Arlington, Massachusetts, c. 1948

Nelson Town Hall c. 1949, Dudley Laufman, accordion, Albert Quigley, fiddle, unidentified piano player

Ralph Page and his Orchestra, Bell's Studio, Peterborough, N.H. c. 1950.
Left to right: Bob McQuillen, Russ Allen, Dick Richardson, "Junior"
Richardson, John Tremblay, and Ralph Page

Dudley Laufman and Friends at the Club 47, 47 Palmer Street, Cambridge
MA, early 1965. Left to right: Jack Sloanaker, Dave Fuller, Dudley Laufman,
Joe Ryan, Jack O'Connor, and Newton F. Tolman

Newt Tolman and
Dudley Laufman,
c. 1965

Bob McQuillen and
"Squeezebox"

Canterbury Dancers and musicians at the Newport Folk Festival, 7/25/65, Sunday evening concert

Canterbury Country Dance Orchestra at the Beers Family Festival,
Petersburgh, NY, c. 1968

Dudley Laufman and Vince O'Donnell, c. 1972

Ted Levin, Art Bryan, and Jack Sloanaker warm up at the Middlesex School Chapel, "Blue Album" recording session, 9/24/71

Canterbury Country Dance Orchestra at the Middlesex School Chapel, "Blue Album" recording session, 9/24/71. Left to right, Bob McQuillen, Allan Block, Jerry Weene, Dudley Laufman, Nicholas Howe, Ted Levin, Dave Fuller, Art Bryan, Peter Colby, and Jack Sloanaker

F&W RECORDS

PRESENT

THE CANTERBURY
COUNTRY DANCE ORCHESTRA

directed by Dudley Laufman
on a 12" 33-1/3 RPM STEREO LP disc

FEATURING

Money Musk   Chorus Jig   Petronella   Prince William   Coleraine Jig
Huntsman Chorus   Yarmouth Reel   Auretti's Dutch Skipper
and other jigs and reels

$5.00

From **F&W Records** Box 44, Plymouth Union, Vermont 05057

Promotional flyer for *The Canterbury Country Dance Orchestra*, 1972

Grange Dance
Poster, c. 1972

97

Dudley Laufman and friends at a Coffin Factory Dance, 88 Miller Street, Somerville, MA, October 1972

Poster for Fitzwilliam Folk
Festival, 1972

Seated: Dudley Laufman, April Limber, Deanna Stiles.
Standing: Peter Colby, Bob McQuillen, and Art Bryan, c. 1974

Fitzwilliam Folk Festival, 1972. Left to right: Jerry Weene, Dudley Laufman, Jack Sloanaker, and Fred Breunig

Phenix Morris Dancers with Art Bryan and Dudley Laufman, c. 1976

Sylvia Miskoe and Dudley Laufman

Sylvia Miskoe

Jacqueline Laufman and Sophie Orzechowski at the *Welcome Here Again* session, 2016. Steve Booth photograph

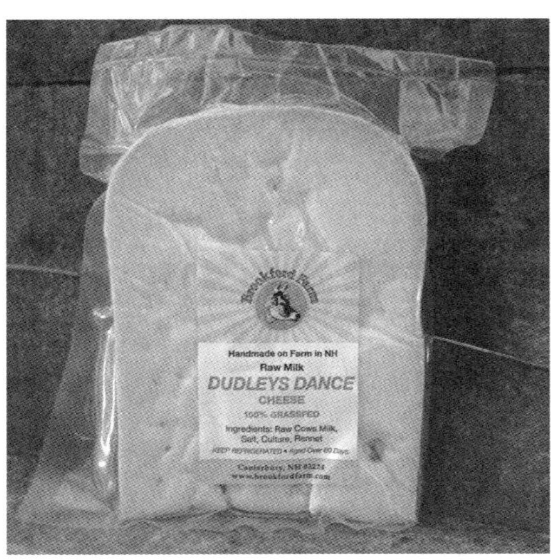

Dudley's Dance Cheese from Brookford Farm, Canterbury, NH, 2022

═11═

Speed the Plow

MORE THAN ONE SORT OF MAGIC was afoot as the tradition of contradance was rekindled during the early 1970s. Rural New England was experiencing a renaissance on the land that was fueled in great part by an infusion of traditional music. Young people were "lighting out for the territories" like fireflies, seeking to put the ideals of Thoreau, Emerson, the Nearings, and agrarian philosopher Liberty Hyde Bailey into personal practice. This "back to the land" movement sprang up throughout the region, and took firm root in the places that fostered the contradance revival. Central and mid-coast Maine, the upland villages of Vermont, and the Pioneer Valley in Massachusetts became centers of self-sufficient farming. In New Hampshire, it was as if a new Homestead Act had taken effect in Seacoast towns, in Tamworth, Sanbornton, Northfield, and Canterbury, and through the long neck of the woods that stretched across through Henniker, Hillsborough, Peterborough, Harrisville, Nelson, Acworth, Alstead, and over the river into Putney and Brattleboro. The impulse to "make a better world" gained force, focus, and function, and became a presence on the Yankee section of the "whole earth."

The back-to-the-land movement has been questioned recently as possibly being escapist in nature, which is a valid point to consider. Almost nothing in America seemed to be functioning well at the time. In May of 1964, folksinger Joan Baez sang at a concert in Madison Square Garden to benefit the presidential campaign of a "peace candidate" who later went on to dramatically escalate the undeclared war in Vietnam. In August that summer, three civil rights workers disappeared in Mississippi and the search for them immediately unearthed the bodies of a number of other, unreported murder victims. The national mood played out in various forms of violence: riots in African-American neighborhoods, the bureaucratic bungling involved in a twenty-year-long special military operation in Southeast Asia, the assassination of two American political leaders and the wounding of a third, and the gunning-down of unarmed protesters on college campuses in Mississippi and in Ohio. America was being weighed in the balance and found wanting.

Following the post-war period of prosperity and the momentum of the early civil rights movement, it became clear that violence and bigotry were ingrained parts of an American life that was still falling far short of the founding principles. The tendency of the general culture and of idealistic youth in particular to expect instant results often translated into quick disillusionment. Although it was not clear at the time, the popular shift into "sex, drugs, and rock 'n' roll" might not have been much more than a stylistic variation on the consumer culture-of-origin. *Playboy* magazine fantasies could be acted out by casually loving the one you were with. Cocaine could be even more effective than Scotch if you were looking for a ticket to oblivion. You could almost spend as much money on a fancy sound system as you could on a used Cadillac. It was hard to see it in the moment, but the times might not have been a-changin' all that much.

While Bob Dylan was "going electric" and Buckminster Fuller was building domes, young people in New England were releasing themselves from "the grid" and attempting to master the skills of old fashioned post-and-beam construction and basic farm and garden husbandry. Given the retrograde trajectory of national events, it seemed clear that some sort of transformative experience would have to be fashioned if the grandchildren of the baby boomers could ever inhabit a world of harmony and decent prospects. Modern culture was failing to address basic human needs and minimal standards of community health and well-being. If answers were to be found to all the crises of conscience that were "blowing in the wind," it was going to take a lot more action than growing long hair and donning a pair of bell-bottomed trousers.

If war was a morally indefensible act, we should remove ourselves from the mechanisms that enabled it. If the economy of Empire was ugly and exploitative, we should live as frugally and "trade" as locally as possible. If our dependence on foreign energy involved the underwriting of toxic dictatorships, we should heat our homes with wood we cut and seasoned ourselves and we should minimize our use of vehicles. If our habits were profoundly unhealthy, we should endeavor to grow our own food and raise enough surplus to give away to "the poor of the parish." For a time (and, in some cases for a lifetime) people chose to see their span of days as a moral crusade, even though this meant a rigorous re-thinking of cultural conditioning and personal habits. The struggle for the redemption of the American soul might be addressed in the forest and the garden, in the kitchen, the barn, and in the shed. You could learn to measure the mark of your convictions in cords of wood and in quarts of homemade canned goods.

The transition from garden variety non-conformity to rural self-sufficiency meant committing to the hard work of hearth and homestead throughout the four seasons. Spring began, not with a trip to the beach, but with a slog through snowy woods on a bright blue morning in February, tapping the sugar bush and cutting down firewood. Marglobe tomato and Merrimack Wonder pepper plants set in peat pots (or egg cartons) were "started" indoors in March. If the snow went off early and the ground thawed, last year's parsnips could be dug up and new peas and lettuce planted in April. If you had critters to put out to summer pasture, you needed to get your fence insulators tacked up before the black flies came out in order to keep from swatting a bug on your forehead with a hammer. Once you were ready to declare the end of the bear market of winter, you could bull ahead and invest all the main garden stuff right off the bat at the end of May: Golden Bantam corn, Blue Lake beans, Boston Marrow and Waltham Butternut squash, and everything else you wanted to plant, from kohlrabi to kale. For two weeks or so in June you devoted to getting your hay in when the sun shone; on days when it showered you thinned your fruit trees, weeded the garden, and shucked and froze your peas. Firewood was split in July if not before, stacked to season up in good shape for the year to follow. In August, there were the fairs to go to, the old home days to participate in, and the woodsheds to fill. Then all of a sudden it was harvest time: the days filled with freezing, canning, pickling, and making cider till the first frost knocked the garden down. Wearing a wool shirt newly fetched out of the closet, you forked your potatoes up out of the sandy loam and into bushel baskets in the waning light before the first snow flurries began to fly.

If you were a nurse's aid or a teacher, a rural mail carrier, or a paralegal, you tried to get the dirt out of your nails and the shit off your shoes before you went to work every day. Pulling a second shift was out of the question when you had a cow to milk. Compliments about the aroma of an aftershave were accepted with a smile, since it was likely the smell of wood smoke that drew attention. No matter how tired you were, no matter how much you grumbled about having too much on your plate, no matter how much you had to risk getting a speeding ticket on the way to the old town hall, all the stress evaporated once you arrived at a contradance. You could hear Art Bryan's tenor voice echoing in your heart: "*This* is what I want to do."

On the surface of it, during the days when Spiro T. Agnew and Abby Hoffman were wrestling across the national headlines, New England might have seemed like an odd place to find common ground. But, as the non-conformist pioneers of the post-World War II era had learned, there was an instinctive respect for conviction of any kind in Yankee life, coupled with a deep distrust of genteel convention. *Oh, they cut a kinda queer show, them young people out on the Potato Road. But, by God, they know how to work. What they do with their lives hain't none of my business. Kinda nice to see 'em bringin' the old Forrest Gardner place back, you know. They got new sills under it and a new roof half done, by the looks. Another winter without being tended to and that old place would have fallen right into the cellar. Woulda been a real shame…*

Not in every case, but in many small towns, a sort of cultural give-and-take evolved in contrast to the conflicts and confrontations that prevailed nationally. When an old Yankee watched the newcomers pruning up an old Blue Pearmain apple tree and bringing back an overgrown pasture into cultivation, he might have thought, well, maybe in the long run my great-grandad knew what he was doing when he didn't kite off to Sacramento in a clipper ship like his older brothers did. Around the same time, when a wild-haired post-adolescent "farmer" dropped himself into a thrift-shop easy chair after a day spent attempting to split firewood, he might choose to drop the needle on a Dolly Parton record on the nearby turntable instead of firing up The Doors. Here and there, a few hippies joined the Grange and a conscientious objector got voted in as town moderator, which, when you think of it, actually made a certain amount of sense.

By virtue of his Quaker upbringing, Dudley Laufman could bring a lifetime of deep conviction to the tasks of homesteading. A combination of circumstances illuminated his journey up from Middlesex to the Merrimack. He had felt called to farming at an early age, and he had begun a combined apprenticeship and transformation at Mistwold Farm. He had honed his agricultural skills at Norfolk Aggie, at the Stockbridge School, at Farm and Wilderness Camp, and as a rural handyman in Hillsborough. In the town of Nelson, he had served a sort of cultural apprenticeship with characters like Albert Quigley, Frank Upton, and Newt Tolman and entered into deep friendships with them. These experiences were mortared together with the tenets of pacifism and simplicity that he had been brought up with. By the time he put the roof and chimney on his little house out on Shaker Road, he was both a birthright Quaker and a convinced homesteader.[88]

---

88. In addition to music, Dudley found artistic expression in poetry. His travels, his musicianship, and the vitality of homestead life mixed together with local culture and climate to inspire themes for his verse. See "Two Poems and a Piece" by Dudley Laufman, in this volume, for a sample of his poems.

The role of the contradance revival in this new Yankee springtime fit in to the landscape like an oak peg pounded into a post and beam joint. There was a kind of reconciliation that went on out on the dance floor, propagated by a mixture of tradition, good will, and strong personalities. The new gathering of contradance musicians was nothing if not a first-rate collection of free-range characters. Bob McQuillen might have led the procession in this ragged Virginia reel, a big, bluff ex-Marine with long white hair sprouting out from under a Bob Dylan cap. He was flanked by Dudley Laufman, outspoken Quaker; Newt Tolman, backwoods aristocrat; Sylvia Miskoe, diminutive force of nature; Joe Ryan, yurt-builder; Vince O'Donnell, civil rights activist wearing a dashiki along the streets of Penacook; Peter Colby, maker of banjoes and flintlock rifles; and Deanna Stiles, a new age earth mother living in a shed fashioned from the crate in which Lindbergh's *Spirit of St. Louis* was shipped back to the States from Paris in 1927. When that sort of a karmic delegation strode into an old dance hall lugging a collection of antique instruments and preparing to play tunes that the audience's great-grandparents had courted to, the local folks had little choice but to step out on the dance floor and see what might transpire. More often than not the verdict came back: "Pretty damn' good!"[89]

In his own way, consciously or not, Dudley became something of an itinerant preacher. In twenty years of travels through the watersheds of the Connecticut and the Merrimack, he had soaked up a good deal of Yankee dance tradition. When the spirit moved him beyond those ports of call, his compass often seemed to point him nor' by nor'east along the coast of Maine. The country of pointed firs is almost as large as the rest of New England combined, and the conjoined energy of musical renaissance and the back to the land movement covered an enormous amount of ground between Kittery and Calais in the 1970s. In Maine, as elsewhere in New England, the

---

89. Or, as Chuck Berry once put it, "C'est la vie say the old folks, it goes to show you never can tell."

post-Woodstock reality for many musicians was that live music was synonymous with bars, and, over time, bars became synonymous with headaches. Traditional country dancing seemed to be a healthy distance removed from the stale beer sort of rock scene where the sound of your own wheels was likely to make you crazy.

Greg Boardman was a student at Colby College at the time, a musician whose journey had run from rock 'n' roll bands to bluegrass and old-timey music. He took up the fiddle soon after seeing the British roots rock band Fairport Convention play at the King's Rook Coffeehouse in Ipswich, Massachusetts. His musical journey rapidly intersected with Scotch-Irish and French-Canadian traditions. It was about that time that Dudley Laufman gave a day-long musical workshop followed by a contradance at Bowdoin College. Young musicians were drawn in from all across Maine, and a cassette bootlegged out of the workshop was duplicated and circulated all over the state.

Greg remembers:

> *I first heard about Dudley's dances from a woman I*
> *met in college. They sounded heavenly to me, but when*
> *I asked her to go to one with me sometime she refused.*
> *She shared the opinion going around that he was*
> *rather gruff and often impatient with dancers and did*
> *not want to put herself in an uncomfortable position.*
> *I enjoyed several dances thereafter and had too much*
> *fun to notice anything of the like. Once I traveled with*
> *friends to a dance in Blue Hill, where I had the joy*
> *of being invited to play along for the first time, once*
> *I got there and offered my services. Just his button*
> *accordion and my fiddle, no PA, maybe fifty dancers.*
> *Really nice acoustics in the old town hall, bitter cold*
> *winter's night, the moon visible in the circular window*
> *through the ceiling. Dudley likes to tell the story of me*
> *turning to him between dances at one point and saying*
> *"You're not so bad!"*

Dudley's style and personality contrasted with Ted Sannella's easy-going approach; both were popular, both contributed much to the revival of traditional dance, and both attracted partisans to their respective interpretations of the form. In Maine, in particular, Dudley represented a unique mixture of talents and convictions, coupling contradance, musicianship, poetry, and a hands-on commitment to homesteading. Through his friendship with Joe Ryan of the Fiddler's Choice village just north of Canterbury, Dudley connected with Bill Copperthwaite, iconic philosopher, educator, back-to-the-lander, and owner/occupier of an enormous yurt tucked into a remote bay off the grid and far away from the beaten path up near Machiasport.

On the one hand, Dudley was a charismatic who tended to see things his way, and on the other he seemed to combine a Bohemian spirit with a deep, abiding, and surprisingly conventional Quaker faith. Greg Boardman recalls:

> *One memorable trip was spent with him and*
> *[his 2nd wife] Patty, plus our friends Bob Childs,*
> *Taylor Whiteside, and Doug and Elaine Protsick on*
> *Vinalhaven and North Haven. One of the many little*
> *gigs we had was a visit to the elementary school on*
> *North Haven, doing a classroom program and dance*
> *with the kids. We played and sang before the dance, one*
> *song being my introduction to [Quaker] George Fox,*
> *words by Sydney Carter, to the tune of Monk's March.*
>
> *I remember being shocked that such an outright*
> *spiritual song was being sung in a public school, and*
> *by the image and exhortation of the title character, in*
> *his old leather britches and his shaggy, shaggy locks,*
> *to "walk in the Light," and him being told "you are*
> *walking in the glory of the Light." I caught on to the*
> *chorus and joined in, singing through my tears. Here*
> *in song, I felt, was my heart's desire, to be fully myself,*
> *in the wonder, adventure and security of some kind of*
> *light. Within a year or two after that I came to see the*

event as one of a series of seminal events, which led me
out of the frightening life of meaninglessness I feared
was my destiny into an immersion into the kingdom of
God in Christ. I remain forever grateful.[90]

There was a goodly amount of redemption inherent and available in the work; you could play it, you could dance to it, and you could simply close your eyes and feel it wash over you in the living presence of wherever you were taken by the grace in the music. In Maine, folksinger Dave Mallett's phrase, the countryside was "greenin' up real good," and music was a major influence in the sense of new possibilities that was dawning across the Yankee landscape. Mallett, Tom Rush, Gordon Bok, and the Canterbury Country Dance Orchestra were prominent among the hundreds of New England musicians who lent inspiration, energy, and craft to the traditions being hewn by hand out in the Yankee hinterlands. In light of the convictions and experiences of that time and from those places, there is much more than music that meets the ear in the wonderful recordings that were made back in the days of the rural New England folk revival. They are still well worth a listen in any season.

---

90. Author's conversations with Greg Boardman, May 2022.

≡12≡

Itinerant Musicians License

BY THE MID-1960s, Dudley Laufman had already devoted the better part of a decade to establishing himself as the leading inheritor and proponent of a long-neglected New England dance tradition. He was logging a thousand miles a week in an itinerary that took him throughout all the corners and nooks of the Yankee landscape. Dudley found himself in the position of being the master and commander of a ship in a bottle: the wonderful old windjammer of country dance that had largely been dormant for a century. As time passed, a certain alchemy began to assert itself, and he felt drawn into an artistic identity that was hundreds of years and several thousand miles removed from Shaker Road. He started to envision himself as being the same sort of traveling dance master that had frequented the Scottish lowlands in the nineteenth century and, mayhap, even before then.

Despite the veneer of a Calvinist past, the Scots can be a profoundly mystical people and the itinerant dancing master of highland and glen was something of a high priest of the ancient ways.

"The dancing dominie…fixes on a barn in some *clauchan*[91] to show forth in; he can both fiddle and dance, at the same time; he

---

91. An old Scottish term for a village.

can cut double-quick time…so the young folk in the neighborhood doff their clogs and put on their dancing pumps, and off they go…" according to a lowland account of 1824. A writer in 1773 tells us that "Reels, strathspeys, country-dances, and hornpipes here are practiced…The attachment of the people of Scotland of every rank, and particularly the peasantry, to this amusement is very great. After the labors of the day are over, young men and women walk many miles, in the cold and dreary nights of winter, to these country dancing-schools, and the instant that the violin sounds a Scottish air, fatigue seems to vanish."[92]

In those fine olden times, the itinerant dance master made his way through a circuit of towns of all sizes, teaching steps while playing a smallish fiddle tucked onto his forearm as he danced around in barns and halls. The image began to dominate Dudley Laufman's thinking. In relatively short order, this vision became a sort of personal identity for him as much as it was an historical re-creation. He asked his wife Patty to sew him a deep-pocketed green velvet jacket trimmed with gold, he took to wearing a gilded sash, and up he went to David Coburn's Vintage Fret Shop in Ashland to have a small, three-string fiddle made out of an old fiddle neck and a Royal Jamaica cigar box. He began to act out a part that in another age would have seen him traveling from town to town like a pied piper or a conjurer, casting a musical spell while convening a village in celebratory instruction, or perhaps it was instructive celebration.[93]

The centuries of civilized Christendom might have been moving out of their late teens, but the latter-day country dance master drew from a bag of tricks handed down from the most ancient of days.

---

92. J. F and T. M. Flett, *Traditional Dancing in Scotland* (Nashville: Vanderbilt University Press, 1966), 28.

93. Although his vision was particularly idiosynchractic, Dudley was not alone in this regard. More than one vagabond found himself ordering his life completely around a schedule and an itinerary of contradances. Jack Perron's immersion in the world of contradance, and that of others in that period, is described in Richard Nevell's *A Time To Dance*, (New York; St. Martin's Press, 1977), 115–123.

Runes took the form of tunes on nights when the joy of movement flowed in a rhythmic tidal pull of hormones and harmonies under the glow of a rising May moon. The fiddle skirled and the dancers whirled and the fiddler cantered his way around the hall. Stars reeled in their courses above a rolling hayloft and the waves of a featherbed in a room over the tavern. Then it was up in the morn with the roosters; way, hey, and away we go, down the road with a bellyful of porridge and the fiddle in the pack, on to the next village full of rugged, stomping swains and, of course, the comely lasses. Amidst the bustle and swing of waists and hems in an old hall, a pair of eyes could easily be seen to signal to "come hither." In a way it was pure magic, and in a way it was skirting well across the borders of reality.

There were boundaries that could be easily blurred when the tunes you were hearing in your head were centuries old before they were ever written down, and they hadn't been written down until a couple of hundred years before you were born. If ever there was fertile ground for odd visitations of spirits and come-agains, of the manifestation of haints and saints, and for the suspension of time and place, surely this was it. The ghosts of musicians long past sat in on your internal soundtrack while you learned their work well enough to fill the empty seats with living generations of fiddlers and pipers. All well and good, but when you filled out your tax forms, what the hell were you supposed to write in the space labeled "Occupation"?

In 1971, Jim Rooney wrote a book called *Bossmen*, a vivid exploration of the pivotal role of past-keeping played out in the lives of Kentucky bluegrass musician Bill Monroe and Chicago blues icon Muddy Waters. Dudley Laufman could easily have been added to that good company. Like the other men, he had taken a rich but neglected art form, preserved its integrity, stamped it with his own character, and put together a compelling roster of young musicians who began to renew and revive the old tunes. Like them, he had taught his version of a traditional idiom to a new generation. Like them, too, he had a strong ego and a demanding personality, and like them he took on the role of ringmaster in something of a traveling musical circus. For these and other traditional musicians, fame, recognition, and popularity brought along with them a complex set of unintended personal and professional consequences.

When Dudley began to establish himself as an up-and-coming caller, he took pains to honor the tradition of "sitting in" that he had learned from old timers. Fostering new musicians was as much a principle as a practice in his eyes. Art Bryan established himself as a walk-on and then became a mainstay of the group. Vince O'Donnell had come aboard after sitting in at a poetry session in Canterbury. Jack Perron, Taylor Whiteside, April Limber, and Jane Orzechowski were among others who began their long roles with the orchestra more or less by chance. When talented flautist Deanna Stiles asked Sylvia Miskoe if she knew of a band where she could stretch out her playing style, Sylvia suggested that she give the Canterbury group a try. Dudley could be flexible with his musicians, but he could also lay down the law about form and practice, particularly in regard to the playing of medleys of tunes, which, by and large, he did not believe in.

A number of complications were musical, but beneath the music were a host of cultural dynamics that were playing out in the 1960s and 1970s in every corner of America, and particularly on the rural landscape. The revival of folk music, the stirrings of the back-to-the-land movement, and the revolution in culture that seemed for a time to have culminated in the Woodstock Music Festival in upstate New York all suddenly introduced a wild new set of variables onto the "scene." In the 1970s, a new generation began flocking to the countryside, imagining the joys of living off the land but often oblivious to the dynamics, the subtleties, and the sacrifices inherent in rural life. For years, every summer, a few shaggy stragglers had hitchhiked up into the hinterlands; now Volkswagen buses full of them were arriving well ahead of the seasonal clouds of black-flies. What resulted, in many cases, bore less resemblance to a pilgrim's progress than it did to *The Magical Mystery Tour*, the Beatles' colorful yet incoherent TV special of 1968.

For about a decade, "Dudley Dances," as they came to be known, had been modest gatherings of old-timers, summer people, farmers, church secretaries, seasoned dancers, and here and there a few bewildered newcomers. Several of his musicians were young city people, yet one of his fiddlers was a logger, his banjo player made replicas of Revolutionary-era muskets, and almost everybody involved was raising their own food and heating their homesteads with wood. Then, during the late-1960s, a new influx of day-trippers, New-Age nomads, and back-to-the-landers flowed up into New Hampshire like a fleet of floating yurts bobbing up the Piscataqua on the coming flood.[94] For the most part, the mixture of beards and paisley with hunting vests and snowmobile boots drew forth the good nature of all concerned, but there was always the chance that a local person would take offense at the smell of burning leaves in June, or that an advocate of peace-and-love would attempt to make the world a better place by telling other people what to do. Every dance was different; every combination of musicians and dancers was dynamic in the moment, and much depended upon the instincts and intangibles convened by the caller. More often than not, Dudley's blend of charisma and command carried the day.

Dudley's musical philosophy was a unique mix of structure and tolerance. He had definite ideas about what was what; he hadn't sprouted under the influence of Ralph Page and Newt Tolman for nothing. His Canterbury Country Dance Orchestra members were all top-flight musicians, as any listening of the Middlesex Chapel recordings will testify. But the demand for dances was high. Not all of his recording group could make it around the forested flanks of Mount Monadnock, down across the expanse of northern Maine, or up from the teeming squares of Cambridge on any given night. He adapted by welcoming any musicians who showed up at a dance with an instrument and wanted to play along, in the same way that he had been allowed to sit in with established outfits in the days when he was learning. Quite often, a new musician was a guitar

---

94. Joe Ryan was among a group of musicians and back-to-the-landers that gathered in a community of yurts located just north of Canterbury in Northfield, New Hampshire, that became known as "Fiddler's Choice."

player, likely someone who knew the Bob Dylan songbook from cover-to-cover but had never heard of *M.M. Cole's 1000 Fiddle Tunes*.[95] As Vince O'Donnell later remembered: "There's nothing like sitting next to somebody else who knows more than you do… that's such a great way to get better. The welcoming experience is fundamental." The nurturing of young musicians was second nature to Dudley Laufman.

In the flow of any given dance, Dudley might have found himself occupying a crucial but not always comfortable position as both a keeper of tradition and an advocate for flexibility. Young transplants from the city fell readily into hybrid steps that owed much to the flow of rock 'n' roll dances, and Dudley became an advocate for these impromptu variations on the old forms. Over the years, country dancers had borrowed or invented flourishes that came from African-American plank and "buck-dancing," French-Canadian figures, and Irish steps, and more recent times had seen bits and pieces of the Charleston and the Lindy hop grafted onto dance steps around the old halls. As the 1970s unfolded, many country dancers added twists and turns that had originated in bebop music and record hops two decades earlier.

As the tape of the Coffin Factory dance illustrates, a number of contradance enthusiasts had focused on becoming first-rate instrumentalists at a relatively early age. Once they achieved confidence and virtuosity, some found little patience for people whose idea of a good time in folk music was listening to endless versions of "Freight Train" through the course of a long night. Some wanted to trace their musical roots back across the water to the other Tunbridge, the one with deep wells in it instead of a covered bridge and a country fair. Many sought a connection to ancient traditions of Morris dances, maypoles, and madrigals.

---

95. Originally published as *Ryan's Mammoth Collection* by the Elias Howe Company of Boston in 1883; still in print today from the M.M. Cole Company of Chicago. An amazingly rich source of traditional tunes.

In the British Isles, young musicians like The Chieftains, Steeleye Span, the Watersons, and the folk music iteration of Fairport Convention were delving into the barrows of English tunes and songs, and they seemed to be making a good living while doing it. Fred Breunig, Randy Miller, and Jack Perron spoke with Dudley about recording an album that might be somewhat more in line with what was going on in England at the time. The result, in 1973, was a record called *Itinerant Musician's License*,[96] which sought to expand and concentrate the vision of the music, primarily along the lines of its roots in the British Isles.

About a year later, Peter Colby approached Dudley with the idea of a more compact iteration of the Canterbury sound. This time, the thought was to reduce the group to six players: Dudley; Pete and his partner, fiddler April Limber; Deanna Stiles, a brilliant flute player; and old friends Art Bryan playing guitar and Bob McQuillen on the stately, rolling piano. The common denominator here was to be virtuosity, the thinking went, and, along with that, a more focused strategy around recording.

A combination of factors had begun to influence the life of the Canterbury Country Dance Orchestra. In a few short years, young musicians had begun transitioning from lives as free musical spirits into people with rent to pay, cars to buy, marriages committed to, and the need to establish a career as a means to achieve economic survival, if not security. There were questions about financial matters; artistic success was all well and good, but there seemed to be money being made in traditional music, as has been noted, particularly among the English folk groups. It was felt by some that with the establishment of more focus and equity, the members of the group could "do better."

Dudley's authority was challenged in this regard, and the dynamics of the group shifted from being a large and informal ensemble under Dudley's direction to a set of six core musicians that

---

96. *Itinerant Musicians License*, Dudley Laufman, Fred Breunig, Jack Perron, and Randy Miller. No label, 1973.

was attempting to move towards a more collective form of decision-making. The group decided to venture over to the Hudson Valley in March of 1974 to record fifteen tunes that would be released as the album *Swinging On A Gate*.[97] They came to the dooryard of Front Hall Records in Voorheesville, New York, run by Bill and Andy Spence, who had already released several traditionally oriented recordings and would go on to produce dozens more over the course of the coming decades.

As had been designed, the choice of material was imaginative and engaging, the sound was rich, tight, and stirring, and the resulting recording has aged well over the years. For the younger musicians, this was an exercise in precision to the point of perfection of craft, and thus was an opportunity to showcase their considerable talents and capacities.[98] Yet, for Dudley, the recording studio process turned into tedium, and so at one point he ambled off to Albany to take a break from the proceedings. Despite the friction that had been involved in its conception, the latter-day listener can come away with a conclusion borrowed from the title of one of the tunes in the piece: still, they say, she's kinda pretty.

The Canterbury group had a fascinating experience in the Cambridge studios of WGBH in Boston, during an appearance on the nationally broadcast *Morning Pro Musica* radio program hosted by Robert J. Lurtsema. Unbeknownst to many of his later listeners, Lurtsema had long been a player in the Boston folk music revival, emceeing a folk radio show called *Folk City USA* on WCRB, acting as art director for the *Broadside* magazine of Boston in the mid-60s, and being well-known as a "regular" at the Unicorn Coffee House on Boylston Street.

---

97. *Swinging On A Gate*, Dudley Laufman and the Canterbury Country Dance Orchestra, Front Hall Records FHR-03, 1974.

98. The album had long been out of print when Art Bryan recently saw to it that it could be re-released in a restored CD version. It remains a remarkable piece, one well worth seeking out.

His WGBH program was about a year old when he invited the Canterbury group to appear in 1972; he would go on to broadcast his well-renowned classical music hour for decades. Perhaps remembering their encounter in Fiddler Beers' woodlot, Dudley and Robert J. engaged in a bit of a verbal jousting of the sort that often plays out between city and country folk: the urbanite asking questions based upon assumed but uninformed reality, and the rural person reacting to the assumptions rather than the questions. The music, however, was superb: "Rickett's Hornpipe," a stately, soaring "Greensleeves Jig," the sweet, moving "Shepherd's Wife," "The Nutting Girl," and the old Morris tune "Dearest Dickey."

The six-person *Swinging On A Gate* lineup made one of its final appearances on August 16, 1975, at the wedding of Art and Laurie Bryan. Peter Colby kicked the day off with a rousing ragtime autoharp rendition of Blind Boone's "Carrie's Gone To Kansas City." After the ceremony in the Episcopal Chapel at the Dublin School, all gathered for a dance that featured the Canterbury group with the addition of Laurie Bryant playing the bodhran, the traditional drum of Celtic music. The "Gate" album was among the few recorded legacies of April Limber and Pete Colby. Both musicians died tragically in 1988 after making one additional CD with Bob McQuillen as "New England Tradition."[99] Limber and Colby had been teaming up with Bob since 1978, often playing at the dances in Francestown Town Hall called by Todd Whittemore. When all was said and done, despite the vicissitudes of interpersonal dynamics, this six-person iteration of the Canterbury Country Dance Orchestra made wonderful music.

Emphasis can naturally be placed on the tapes and recordings that were made and treasured over the years, or those that have been discovered and archived more recently. Yet the heart and soul of contradance music was, and still is, a repeating roster of weekly, monthly, and seasonal dances. The bulk of the group's performance schedule was made up of individual dances and the relationships

---

99. *Farewell To The Hollow*, The New England Tradition CDWM 9860, 1991.

that began or were nurtured within them. Over time, Nelson, Canterbury, Tamworth, and Franconia had been among the most reliable ports of call, but the constellation of dances included East Concord (later Boscawen), Randolph, Sanbornton, East Andover, West Hopkinton, up near Belfast, Maine, down to Concord and Amherst, Massachusetts, and over to Cornwall and other points in Connecticut. Over time, trips to the Midwest and West Coast helped spread the tradition. Scores of great musicians and friends contributed their talents, many of whom would never set foot in a recording studio. Fiddlers, piano players, flautists, and other players participated at schools, churches, community functions, granges, sap houses, barn dances, and weddings to comprise the larger hinterland community that played for "every country dancer."

Each dance took on a life of its own, based largely on the character of the hall and the aura of its setting. Many of the country dance halls of New England had been in service for well over a century. Nelson Town Hall, the second floor of the Boston YWCA, Huggins Barn in Tamworth, Alex Bernhard and Myra Maman's majestic old barn in East Andover, Benson's Barn in Saxton's River, Vermont, and the buildings at the Maine Fiddle Camp are a few examples among many. A blindfolded veteran dancer or musician could probably have identified where they were by the unique smell of the air and the distinctive creak of the floor over the floor joists of an old building.

When it was time to play the "Virginia Reel," a caller like Willie Woodward would get the group lined up inside the hall and then lead them outdoors, off the porch, and onto the lawn or village green, dancing on into the dark and then back again. When a wild thunderstorm slammed over Bridgewater Hill in the 1980s and took the electricity out at the old Town House, a dozen guys deployed their pickups around the windows and turned their headlights on. Willie ratcheted his calling up a notch, old B&M Railroad man Spud Dicey leaned hard into his well-worn fiddle, and the dance went right on ahead in the downpour, just as slick and as snug as could be. Likewise, when the lights went out in the middle of a dance at the stone church in Lincoln, Massachusetts, someone ran home and fetched back a handful of candles so the dance could continue. It is still remembered as a romantic night.[100]

The caller and the group were the most obvious influence on the character of a dance, but the tone of the "regular crowd" in a given town was as important as the sound of the music. Up on Bridgewater Hill, the prevailing atmosphere was set by the local farm family of Stanley and Nina Huckins and by the flock of retired ministers and their wives who contributed to the summer population. Nelson could be said to be a bit rougher venue. The Woodchopper's Ball over in Jaffrey was a downright rowdy collection of loggers who were often in their cups; one night a few of the boys got themselves elevated up on the roof of a car and stomped it down pretty flat, right in time with the music. When you went to a dance at Fiddler's Choice in Northfield, you were out amongst the hippies, plain and simple; smoke 'em if you got 'em. In contrast, a Unitarian church basement in Massachusetts would be festooned with peace posters and the refreshments there were likely to be no stronger than lemonade and tea.

Up about seventy miles south of Quebec City was Lysander's Pavilion in the town of Inverness, with a crowd of Irish descent who all spoke French and loved to dance in squares, as Dudley recalls. Quadrilles were the coin of the realm there, with calls in both English and French, and "St. Anne's Reel" was the iconic equivalent of "Petronella" to the south. In one manner of thinking, Inverness could be seen as being at the northern boundary of true New England country dancing; taking another view, you could think of Concord, New Hampshire, or Chicopee, Massachusetts, as being at the southern end of "the real thing" of French-Canadian dance. Let the *bons temps rouler*.

A writer for the *Christian Science Monitor* attended one of Dudley's dances in 1973, and described the experience: "Most folks

---

100. Author's personal memory of Bridgewater Hill; the Lincoln remembrance is from the *Roaring Jelly Turns 50* video on the NEFFA website.

who have even a spark of the country pulse within them find scuffing to jigs and reels a kind of poetry in motion. The essence of the dance lies in the fact that it is a non-competitive activity, one in which it is nearly impossible to remain self-centered." Dudley is quoted in the piece: "Joy comes as the dancer stops dancing to the calls and starts dancing to the music."[101]

The hustle and bustle of conversation, the random notes of tuning, and the hiss of the heat pipes all receded when a caller like Dudley intoned: "All right, sets together for 'Money Musk.' This is a triple minor proper dance, active couples turn partners once and a half around, below one couple, forward six and back and so forth… here we go!"[102] Then an exclamatory chord on the accordion, the romp of the piano, and, indeed, off they went.

Standing outside in the dark to crack a beer or to free up some belt space, you could feel the living soul of an old hall, with the light glowing out of the old windows like a jack o'lantern, the fiddle keening away like a grasshopper in the dark, and the rhythmic tread of the dancers set by the stalwart left hand of the piano player. Silhouettes of tall dark pines loomed up in the night, framing the twitch of a million stars seen from rural vantage points miles removed from the murk of neon lights. When your arms were empty and you had nowhere to go, there was no need to have a lonely heart in the north country. A contradance was a place where you could not only come on out and catch the show, and you could also be a part of it.[103]

---

101. *The Christian Science Monitor*, Arts & Entertainment section, September 19, 1973.

102. Dudley Laufman entry on the Ted Sannella memory page of the Monadnock Folklore Society website.

103. A tip of the cap to The Band's "W. S. Walcott Medicine Show."

⇒ 13 ⇐

In the Tradition

Classrooms, Camps, and the Belle of the Contradance

DUDLEY HAD THE ADVANTAGE of living in proximity to the progressive and relatively well-funded public schools of Concord, New Hampshire. His personality and his idiom put him on a level far above the quality and the impact of the average "music appreciation" experience that was made available in the classroom. By and large, the kids responded enthusiastically to the opportunity to learn music at the personal level. "They really like it because it introduces them to a tradition most of them aren't even aware exists, and a lot of them have never seen a live musician before," Dudley explained to author Richard Nevell. "I show them the melodion, take it apart, and show them the inside. Then we do dances and singing games, and I try not to talk down to them. I just treat them like anybody else, as I would at any dance. The half hour in the classroom gets the same treatment as three hours in the dance hall. It has to be a meaningful and a worthwhile experience. I try to make it so it's not like a classroom, try to forget that. It is educational to some degree, but I'm primarily interested in social content."[104]

---

104. Richard Nevell, *A Time To Dance* (New York: St. Martin's Press, 1977), 108.

Dudley was representing a tradition that had the benefit of a two-hundred-year-old tailwind in America, one that generations of local kids had grown up with, some of them falling asleep on piles of coats in the dance halls, some of them remembering "kitchen junkets" where the kitchen furniture, and sometimes even the cookstove, was pushed aside to make room for dancers, musicians, and a caller. Those sorts of country dance traditions had long disappeared from suburban America, but families and memories were still living in a different frame of reference in northern New England, even in a state capital. Dudley played at the Rumford, Eastman, Conant, and Kimball schools in the Concord system, and in classrooms in Keene, Wolfeboro, and other New Hampshire cities and towns.

One day in 1988, Dudley was working with a group of second-graders at the Conant School when a little girl approached him and asked if he knew a fiddler named Dick Richardson. "The only Dick Richardson I ever knew taught me how to play the fiddle," answered Dudley. The little girl was named Karen Langley, and she was Richardson's granddaughter. Her mother brought in a box of photographs of the old fiddler, one of which Dudley had taken himself, years before, when Dick was one of the mainstays in Ralph Page's band. One thing led to another, and Dudley went to work with Corinne Nash, Dick's daughter, to compile and digitize recordings and to compose a book about him titled *Dick Richardson, Old-Time New Hampshire Fiddler* in 1992.[105] The restoration and digitization of the Dick Richardson tapes was the first collaboration between Dudley and Gerry Putnam of Cedarhouse Sound and Mastering of North Sutton, New Hampshire. Gerry was struck by Dudley's desire to ensure a lasting legacy for the material, and by his growing comfort with the studio. He remembers that "the more we worked on the project, the easier it got."

During a period of various gatherings and solo performances, two other formal recordings were made in the 1970s and 1980s.

---

105. Dudley Laufman and Corrine Nash, *Dick Richardson, Old-Time New Hampshire Fiddler* (Keene: Historical Society of Cheshire County, 1992).

The first was *Canterbury Folk At The Belknap Mill,*[106] recorded in the 1970s in the building erected in 1823 on the banks of the Winnipesaukee River in Laconia, now the oldest unaltered brick textile mill in the nation. Dudley played concertina, his second wife Patty played the drum, Barry Draper played horn, Gretchen Draper sang, and Richard Gehrts played banjo. The group put together fourteen cuts that covered Handel and Haydn tunes, Scottish and English jigs and reels, Irish music-hall fare, and even a few songs from the western prairies. The recording was made available only on cassette tape. The old brick hall had a bit of a dry sort of sound, Dudley recalls, yet it was a lovely place to play. The session was completed in a single day.

In 1981, Dudley and a group of friends ventured into the stately headquarters of the New Hampshire Historical Society and recorded an album called *Shake A Leg: Canterbury Folk at the Marble Palace.*[107] Dudley played concertina and Patty played drum; they were joined by Barry Draper, Lui Collins, Martha Wiederhold, Dick Nevell, and Carl Jacobs. They set down a lively baker's dozen tunes, including two Bob McQuillen originals, a Scottish piper's tune from the trenches of World War I, and an old Child ballad. All were recorded in the superb acoustics of the marble rotunda that had been designed by Daniel Chester French and built in 1911 of the materials used in the Library of Congress.

In 1985, members of Dudley's Canterbury Orchestra gathered together to play at the New Hampshire Folk Festival. Feeling that the time was right for a new release, Jack Sloanaker raised the idea of making another CCDO recording. Dudley started making a list of good tunes that he had not previously set on tape. On June 9, 1986, a reconstituted Canterbury Country Dance Orchestra convened once again at the Middlesex School Chapel to record a seventeen-song playlist that was released on cassette under the title *The Belle of*

---

106. *Canterbury Folk At The Belknap Mill,* Dudley Laufman and Friends, c. 1976.
107. *Shake A Leg: Canterbury Folk at the Marble Palace,* Dudley Laufman and Friends, 1981, cassette tape.

the Contradance.[108] Musicians included Dudley Laufman, accordion; Greg Boardman, fiddle, guitar, vocals; Lydia deAmicus Reeve, fiddle; Dave Fuller, accordion, harmonica; R. P. Hale, hammer dulcimer; Cal Howard, piano, bass; Allan McIntyre, melodion, harmonica; Randy Miller, fiddle; Sylvia Miskoe, accordion; Dick Nevell, guitar; Jack Sloanaker, piano, bass; Deanna Stiles, flute, piccolo; Jerry Weene, five-string banjo, fiddle, mandolin; and Taylor Whiteside, fiddle, viola, piano, and balalaika.

Five musicians from the original-era group played, and the nine additional folks included some of the best players in New England. The resulting sound rivaled the tone and tenor of the old "Blue Album" and of *Mistwold.* The cassette culminated in the title song, an original piece composed and sung by Greg Boardman. The playlist was completed and put "in the can" after a single one-day session. At the close of the long day, R. P. Hale put the huge old pipe organ in the chapel through its paces, playing an improvised selection of compositions. On June 31, 1986, these musicians recorded three additional tunes in concert at the Middlesex School, including "Balkan Hills Schottische," "Opera Reel," and "The Green Cockade."

The *Belle of the Contradance* musicians felt justifiably proud of their work on the recording, and Dudley booked the group into a contradance performance at Passim in Harvard Square, the second site of the "Club 47" of folk-revival fame. Dudley anticipated... he'd likely *expected...* that an enthusiastic group of Cantabrigians would show up eager to dance, but times had apparently changed and, at least on that night, he was faced with a meager and lackluster audience who were well outnumbered by the roster of Canterbury musicians. Dudley strode into the kitchen and drafted the food prep and wait staff on the spot and told them to get out on the floor and put their talents to work as dancers. Greg Boardman remembers "And they did. It was great. Dudley could always make it happen!"

---

108. *The Belle of the Contradance*, Canterbury Country Dance Orchestra, F&W cassette tape, 1986.

The large Canterbury Country Dance Orchestra gathered in 1987 to play at the Old Songs Festival in Altamont, New York. In June of 1992, eighteen members of the group got together for a picnic and a reunion session at Middlesex School. Long-time member Dave Fuller passed away three weeks later, and the group played at his service and again in the fall at a dance held in Dave's memory in Carlisle. In January of 1994, the orchestra played in Peterborough for the benefit of New Hampshire Public Radio. That April, they performed for a dance at Jerry Weene's studio in Waltham, Massachusetts, and later that month at the New England Folk Festival. In December, they headlined the Third Saturday dance in Concord, New Hampshire. The group convened in May of 1995 again in Waltham, a year later in May, 1995, in East Concord, New Hampshire, in the wake of a hurricane in the fall of 1996, and then back to Waltham in May of 1999 for a benefit to rebuild the Violin Artisan Studio after a fire.

No artist knows what their popular trajectory will be and so it would have been impossible to predict either Dudley's rise to prominence in the 1960s or his career's ebb in later decades. Over time, he had published a number of books describing the art of calling, and by the 1990s technology had advanced to the point where portable sound systems could be readily obtained at reasonable cost. So, in the act of mentoring dozens of musicians and callers, he had, in effect, been diminishing his own business prospects. Contradance was gaining quickly in popularity throughout the country, as was the number of younger people available to apply for their share of the business. "My reputation as a caller was dwindling; there were a lot of other people doing it," he recalls.

Dudley and his group had long been established as mainstays of the Concord contra and square dances, playing at the Girl Scout House on Walden Street in Concord, Massachusetts, once a month on Sundays in addition to the shindigs held at the Coffin Factory in Somerville. As the years went by, the tastes and expectations of the local dancers began to shift in the direction of more complex dance structures. Many new dancers excelled in high-functioning jobs in academia and in business in nearby Boston and Cambridge. By the

1990s, a number of them were drawn to seek new variations in the old contradance scene, including medleys, changes in tempo, and the introduction of innovative dance forms set to newly written dance tunes. Dudley was subject to a good deal of pressure in this regard; why couldn't he adapt to the stylistic complexities and innovations that were being favored by new dance enthusiasts?

The answer might have been found in a simple understanding of the role of pastkeeper he had seen himself as playing since the days of Harry S. Truman's presidency. He came into a dance hall to teach a tradition, to perform to the best of his ability as he had been taught, and to see to it that the old ways were carefully passed along to the young. As playing medleys became more and more widespread, Dudley, for the most part, held his ground. In his view, and that of some other traditionalists, "If a tune is good enough to start a dance with, it is good enough to stay with all the way." He forcefully cites the hypnotic effect that sets in as a dance proceeds, and the musical power of mantra that can be disrupted by changes in tempo, in key, or in melody. As his friend and fellow traditionalist John Kirkpatrick of Shropshire, England, has stressed, "These tunes were built for constant repetition…if they did not hold many secrets and yield something new each time round, they would not have survived. They demand to be cherished."[109]

Yet there is also a very good case to be made *for* the use of medleys in contradances, and some of Dudley's closest associates and friends held to that tradition as well. Art Bryan has put it this way: "I do like medleys as long as they are *good* medleys. The tunes need to fit together with similar rhythm and phrasing and make a smooth transition from one to another. Key change is often a plus but not necessary. Playing a single tune for an entire dance can seem boring and the change of tunes inserts energy into the dance. There are times when a single tune is appropriate, especially if the tune is special to the dance, as in

---

109. John Kirkpatrick, "Medley Mania," published in *English Dance and Song* magazine, Volume 43, Number 2, 1981.

'Money Musk.'"[110] Bob McQuillen is said to have viewed the subject philosophically, feeling that there were "so many tunes, so little time!"

Dudley's brand of traditionalism was still being properly recognized. One evening, he and his musicians were playing for a wedding reception held at the Fiddler's Green Tavern, a building that had been erected in 1741 in Duxbury, Massachusetts. In the course of the celebration, the group played for dancing, but at other times they receded into playing background music for diners who conversed and chattered socially. At one point, Dudley remembers, the tavern owner (and chef) burst forth from the kitchen to the dining room, drying his hands on his apron, and climbed up to stand on an empty table. He produced an old conch shell, into which he proceeded to blow with a bugling sound that silenced the buzz of the diners. "I hope you know," the innkeeper intoned, "that this is some of the greatest music that has ever been composed! Listen up!" Having said his piece, he returned to the kitchen, conch shell and all. It had been an effective endorsement.

Throughout the course of the 1980s and 1990s, Dudley recorded a number of cassette tapes; one recalling the story of Arthur Hanson, another of interviews with Mary Dart, and a tape of remembrances of Lin Cady's dances over in Sherburne, Vermont, among others. At one point, he called in a group of musicians including Sarah Bauhan, Art Bryan, Carl Jacobs, Vince O'Donnell, and Bob McQuillen and headed off to make a recording at Philo Records in North Ferrisburg, Vermont. The label featured records by folk musicians including Jean Redpath, Dave Van Ronk, Mary McCaslin, and the Boys of the Lough, among many others, so it seemed like a promising port of call. But the recording process proved difficult, the results were incomplete, and a product never materialized.[111]

---

110. Art Bryan in e-mail to the author.

111. Art Bryan recalls that the most unforgettable feature of the experience was watching the recording engineer feed frozen perch that he'd caught through the ice on Lake Champlain the previous winter to a giant cat named "Chuckles." The recorded music he remembers as being "dreadful."

By 1992, Dudley had joined in partnership with Jacqueline Gilman, also of Canterbury, in the duo that they named Two Fiddles. Together, over the course of nearly fifteen years, the couple became major forces in the traditional dance communities of New England. In addition to fiddling and teaching, Jacqueline ably managed the booking and business aspects of the enterprise and designed and illustrated a number of the many books of music, prose, and poetry that Dudley authored. The New Hampshire State Council on the Arts began encouraging more school performances and music lessons by live musicians, and Jacqueline and Dudley increased the scope of their work throughout New Hampshire as well as into the adjoining states of Vermont and Maine. Working as a team, they were able to tend to the majority of the kids in a given group as well as giving individual attention to any who might be lagging behind.

One gray spring morning, after playing for the third-graders of the Greenland, New Hampshire, elementary school, they paid a visit to the grave of Clement Weeks, the chronicler of contradances from the 1780s. By the shores of Great Bay, their two fiddles played the strains of "Black Joak" in memory of the man who had written the dance down for posterity in his songbook centuries before. [112]

The school work fit well with stints at various summer camps throughout New England. For a time, Dudley had been on the staff of Pinewoods Camp, located on thirty-one acres in Plymouth, Massachusetts, and was well-acquainted with its leadership; it was there that he first picked up the concertina. The camp had been begun in 1919 with a founding focus on folk dance and eventually joined in association with the Country Dance and Song Society. Pinewoods Camp organized one of the earlier Morris dance groups in New England; in short order others sprang up elsewhere, including one in Canterbury.

Greg Boardman founded the Maine Fiddle Camp up in Montville, Maine, at the edge of the St. George River. One of his fiddle students attended Alastair Frazier's music camp in California

---

112. Week's manuscript is at the American Antiquarian Society.

and came back with glowing accounts of the experience. It was felt, almost from a point of pride, that a similar resource should be available for students in Maine. Traditional dancing had caught fire in the state, and from its inception the Maine Fiddle Camp attracted a loyal and enthusiastic following of musicians and campers, growing quickly from a start-up of about fifty people to about three hundred in attendance. Dudley and Jacqueline taught both fiddling and calling at the camp, whose influence grew to the point where Dudley could refer to "Lady of the Lake" as "the national anthem of Maine." The camp has recently moved to Pilgrim Lodge in West Gardiner, Maine, on the shores of Lake Cobbosseecontee, with classes in guitar, mountain dulcimer, piano, ukulele, accordion, melodion, mandolin, and harmonica, as well as in three levels of fiddling. More than two dozen of the camp's instructors teach throughout the year, enriching and continuing Maine's characteristically strong and leading role in the revival of traditional music.[113]

In the realm of recorded local get-togethers, April of 1989 saw about two dozen fiddle players convened at Mary Lou Philbin's house, jointly and severally playing more than three dozen tunes under Dudley's direction in *A Gathering of New Hampshire Fiddlers*. A bit later on, with R. P. Hale on hammer dulcimer, Lois Hornbostel on banjo, and his own accordion, Dudley compiled a collection called *Canterbury Revels* that was recorded at a barn up by Sylvia Miskoe's house on Little Pond Road in Concord. He later set down a sixteen-song cassette titled *Canterbury Capers* with Fred Portnoy. Dudley and Jacqueline released a CD called *The Way It Really Sounds At A Barn Dance* as well as a number of instructional tapes and CDs for use by teachers and students of contradance.

The phrase "Dudley Dance" had come to be synonymous with contradance in New Hampshire. Bookings continued across the map: Peterborough, Nelson, Francestown, Boscawen, and East Concord

---

113. Including fiddler Lissa Schneckenburger, whose youthful experience at music camp in California had done much to inspire the founding of the Maine Fiddle Camp.

in New Hampshire; Putney over in Vermont; Northport, near Belfast, and Hiram in Maine; weddings on Squam Lake and down near Monadnock; at a wonderful corn shucking party in Loudon; and at shindigs all over, including regular junkets and musician's get-togethers at Wind in the Timothy on Shaker Road. Dudley played at the St. Paul's School's summer program every year, guiding scores of kids as they wove their ways around the green and the pond on the old campus. Ten miles out in the ocean from Portsmouth lay the Isles of Shoals, once the haunt of seventeenth-century pirate crews but now the site of the Star Island Conference Center, a magical port of call for contradance. In Tamworth, New Hampshire, dances were held for years at Huggins Barn in town; Ned Behr led the gatherings there until the barn was struck by lightning in the 1950s, then the Tamworth Outing Club set things up at Stafford-in-the-Field every Thursday night from eight to midnight. Ned called the squares and Dudley called the contradances. Amy Berrier has been a major force in the continuation of the dance tradition in the town. "Tamworth is a great place; we thought of it as 'Nelson North,'" Dudley remembers.

Peterborough had long been a center of folk music in the Monadnock region of New Hampshire. Dances were held at the town hall, and folk concerts were organized informally in schools and at private homes. In 1975, two teachers at the Well School, Widdie and Jonathan Hall, created The Folkway, a coffeehouse located on Grove Street that soon became the center of gravity for area folk musicians. Singers from around the country made appearances there, as did a host of talented local and regional artists. The vibrant community that grew around the Folkway mourned the passing of Widdie Hall in 1988, and supported the operation of the coffeehouse by volunteers until the venue closed in 1996. The Monadnock Folklore Society has kept its memory alive and has created a lively center of folk music and contradance lore through its concerts, its website, and archival collaboration with the Peterborough Public Library.

In time, Dudley came to favor the technique of leading a dance in *whole sets*, that is, a version of contradance in which there is only one couple active at a time in each set, and their progression to the foot of the set is completed in one fell swoop. This formation was also referred to as an "old time dance" and was particularly useful when a number of newcomers were in attendance. He learned the form from Emerson Lang, and his calling of "The Mousetrap Reel" "(The Gallopede)." There were times when a whole set would be the structure for an entire evening full of novice dancers; as Dudley remembers, "The use of a whole set can save the night."

A broad set of factors have always played into the dynamics that characterize each dance. One gets the impression that country dance started out as a somewhat rugged sort of pastime. Early dancing masters in Scotland had to teach their students to bow and curtsey, to observe some level of gentility, and to "be verra mannerly when lifting your pairtner, no' likes as if ye were drawing a hog oot o' a ditch," and "after the dance you had to take your partner back to her seat, no' throw her away like a hot potato."[114] On this side of the pond, "Lady of the Lake" was seen as a particularly good opportunity for vigorous whirling, and "apple pie for Yankee gals whose aim and ambition has ever been to swing their partners off the floor and right out straight," sometimes launching them airborne right across the broad expanse of an old hall.[115]

Dudley remembers that the old Nelson Town Hall could get pretty loud once people started dancing in ski-boots. A good deal depended upon the tone set by an individual caller, who, on the one hand, might remind folks that "this is a form of courtship and not a football game," and, on the other, might take the attitude that "anything goes as long as you don't kill each other."

Over time, fashions have changed in regard to style and sensitivities have evolved in regard to gender freedom. Terms like "ladies chain" and "gentlemen's line" have had to be re-worked to fit the preferences of the dancers in a given setting. In this regard,

---

114. J. F and T. M. Flett, *Traditional Dancing in Scotland* (Nashville: Vanderbilt University Press, 1966), 25.

115. Ralph Page and Beth Tolman, *The Country Dance Book* (New York: Barnes & Co., 1937), 85 "There now, folks, is what I call real swingin'!"

Dudley notes that seasoned caller David Millstone has adapted by announcing "This is a traditional dance; I'll do the best I can to accommodate, but if I make a mistake, please forgive me." As for himself, Dudley says "I do things gender free. For example, for "Money Musk:" Once and a half around/Below one couple forward six and back/three quarters around forward six again/three quarters around to place/right and left four. No mention of gender. There are whole programs with dances like that. No larks, no ravens. Just get a partner." One might hope that, where tradition meets innovation at a modern dance, a decent amount of good will can be exercised, and that no one, newcomer, old-timer, insider, or "from away," will be treated imperiously as if they were "a hog oot o' a ditch…"

Both Sides of the Pond

ETWEEN DUDLEY LAUFMAN'S CHILDHOOD in the 1930s and the dawn of "the Sixties," modern American music ran the gamut from the Charleston to big-band swing and then on to pop music and rock 'n' roll. During all that time, Dudley was living in a completely different musical world, one made up of *1,000 Fiddle Tunes* and centuries-old editions of *The English Dancing Master*. Since his teenage years, Dudley had steeped himself in rich traditions that had come over to North America from the British Isles. His musical landscape was full of strathspeys and jigs, reels, marches, and quadrilles. Its regional influences were largely Yankee and French-Canadian, yet the ancestral homes for many of the tunes were the rural villages and towns of England, Ireland, Scotland, Wales, and the countryside of France.

In 1969, after his nearly more than two decades as an active musician, Dudley and Patty Laufman had made a pilgrimage to Ireland. Although he packed a harmonica in his luggage, Dudley remembers that he "went there for the agriculture and the architecture." The couple stayed at a B&B on a farm in County Clare and went to two dances, one in a tent featuring an outfit called Kilmurvy's Band, the other featuring a rock 'n' roll group accompanied by a phalanx of chaperoning priests. Dudley looked up Sean Reed, a musicologist who lived in the town of Ennis, taught track and field at the local high school, played pipes and fiddle, and fronted the well-respected Tulla Ceili Band. They were greeted at the door by Reed's foster daughter, a young African-Irish girl who said matter-of-factly in a thick brogue: "Ye've come for himself!"

Dudley traveled to England on four subsequent occasions, drawn to the countryside, the music, and the people he met there. The field of English country dance covers a wide variety of styles, much like the broad diversity to be found in American folk dancing. The realm of the Morris dance is a universe unto itself, and an ancient one at that. Like many Americans, Dudley was intrigued by a tradition that can be traced in written accounts back to the late 1400s and is likely much older. The ritualized set of dance steps, hand movements, marches, and stick-striking seems to have emerged from a blended tradition that included Dutch, Flemish, Spanish, and French practices. There is strong evidence that it sprang from African influences out of the Spanish Netherlands: "Moors" being the root of nomenclature that may have gone from "Moorish" to "Morris" in the haphazard spelling and custom-tailored pronunciation of the English Middle Ages. It seems connected to the ancient cycle of rural celebrations around what is now Christmas, Whitsuntide, May Day, and harvest time. Morris dance has been described as springing from the complex traditions of "unlettered people" as, one might say, do we all.

Whatever its origins, Morris was all the rage in Elizabethan England, where dancing, particularly of jigs, was closely associated with the theatre. William Kempe (c. 1560–c. 1603) was an actor in Shakespeare's troupe who came to fame in early 1600 when he improbably Morris-danced from London to Norwich, a distance of about 110 miles, in the course of nine days that were spread over a span of several weeks.[116] He was apparently accompanied by a drumming pipe player; he wore bells on his ankles, a decorated costume, flourished a sash, and reportedly was met by cheering

---

116. From Wikipedia: https://commons.wikimedia.org/wiki/File:Will_Kemp
 _Elizabethan_Clown_Jig.jpg#/.

crowds on his journey. In addition to producing an illustrated description of his dance across the countryside, he left behind a piece of music called "Kemp's Jig," which was included in John Playford's *English Dancing Master* in 1651.

The rich folk art and tradition that had sprung up in prehistory, flourished though the Middle Ages, and bloomed in Elizabethan England, fell under the attack of Cromwell and his wrongheaded gang of Puritans, who set out to eradicate all forms of ceremonies, celebrations, and seasonality from England, Ireland, Scotland, and Wales.[117] It was in Royalist enclaves that the remnants of the old ways were protected and thus survived, places like the Cotswolds, the north-west of England, and in the Welsh borderlands. Morris dancing lived on in such locations till it was nearly extinguished, along with much in the way of remaining rural folk life, by the Industrial Revolution of the 1800s. The cultural sterility of modern times called for revival of the old ways, and since the mid-twentieth century, this tradition has been living on in scores of latter-day Morris groups (called "sides") that are active throughout the English countryside.

The dancers generally wear all-white outfits arrayed with sets of jingling bells worn above the ankles, and topped with showy hats that are often decorated with flowers. They are accompanied by costumed musicians playing accordions, flutes, and fiddles. The troupe might include a "fool" as well as a person dressed in a hobby-horse costume, with other features and props developed in local tradition. The steps are energetic and flowing, often including some form of percussion by stick-striking. They lend themselves, in the wandering William Kempe tradition, to marching from place to place in an old town, where a day of Morris dancing often climaxes in the pulsing glow of the local pub.

So it was that Dudley struck up a lifelong friendship with a man named Johnny Wipple, who played with the White Horse Morris group from Warminster, Wiltshire, where he specializes

---

117. Not to mention Massachusetts Bay.

in traditional Border and Cotswold dancing.[118] Johnny played "a humungous button accordion," Dudley had his trusty Hohner with him, and the two men hit it off immediately. Dudley gave Johnny a copy of the newly released *Mistwold* album. Sometime later, after he'd listened to it, Wipple signaled his delight at the record when he greeted Dudley at the Cross Keys pub by saying "Where'd you get them great chunes?" At the Chippenham-Laycock Folk Festival, the White Horse group joined in with other musicians and dancers. Dudley picked up several songs there, including "The Farmer's Boy" and "Clementine," drawn from the old Welsh tune "Cym Rhondda."

While in England, he invited the Bampton Morris group to come over the water to appear at the Canterbury Fair. Dudley had learned Morris dancing at Pinewoods Camp and later helped start three groups in Canterbury: the Phenix Morris Dancers, then a group of youngsters calling themselves the Morris Minors, and later a Canterbury Morris group for adults.

A visit to Abbots Bromley in the English Midlands, north of Birmingham, was a particularly memorable experience for Dudley. He took a train to Tamworth from Heathrow Airport, then walked six miles through the countryside to the village of Abbotts Bromley. The community is known, among other things, for its ancient "Horn Dance" that takes place on Wakes Monday, the day following Wakes Sunday, the first Sunday after the fourth of September each year. The dance, performed by twelve members of a local Morris side, takes the form of a full-day's march through various points in the countryside, with periodic stops to engage in a dance that features six sets of reindeer antlers that are shouldered by the dancers. How long the dance has been going on is not known; there is written reference in 1686 to the horns, and to the hobby horse quite a bit

---

118. From the group's 2022 website: "We practice every Wednesday during the winter months from September through to April in Wylye Village Hall starting at 7:30 p.m. We finish at 9:30 when we usually drift along to the pub for a drink and a chat and sometimes some music. The sessions are free, very sociable and a great way of keeping fit. So why not give it a go?"

earlier, in 1532. The fair on Wakes Monday is first mentioned in writing in 1221. The antlers themselves are even more ancient; carbon dating of a fragment from one of them takes it back to the year 1065. Tradition has it that the event began when a local lord granted hunting rights on his land to the common people and the dance may be in the nature of a commemoration of his generosity. Given the late point in the season, it might also have served as a rite of harvest fertility.[119] We may never know, and it may never matter, as long as the traditions are honored for the joys and the sense of community that they can bring to all those who allow themselves to fall under their spell.

The old horns are displayed in a place of honor in the church of St. Nicholas, taken down early in the morning as the long day of dance procession began with the music of an accordion, augmented by a triangle on the off-beat of the tune "The Cock of the North." The first dance commenced right outside the church, then the group went on to a pub, and from there to a farmhouse where the farmer joined in the dance, and then the whole lot went into the house for breakfast. Back they came out, full of good oatmeal, and were joined in procession through town, playing from a repertoire that included "Yankee Doodle," "The Cock of the North," and "Yellow Submarine."[120] Eventually they all reached the lord mayor's house for a dance and a meal, then back on the road to various stops, including, late in the long day, at the entrance to a public house where the pub-keeper danced with the group before inviting them to come on in and wet their whistles. From the pub it was just a short jog to the close of the event at the church, where the old sets of horns were hung reverentially for another year after a minor ceremony. The townspeople shook hands, embraced, and went home. Dudley was

---

119. Tolerantly referred to by the local Anglican priest, Rev. Simon Davis, bless him, as pagan with a small p.

120. Among many tunes used in Morris Dancing are: "Constant Billy," "Haste to the Wedding," "The Nutting Girl," "The Black Joak," "Bobby Shaftoe," "Roxburghe Castle," "Dearest Dicky," and "Bobbing Joe."

staying with a local farmer, who drew him a mug from a barrel of homemade red ale that he kept in the yeasty atmosphere of the old barn. As Dudley's tongue took the measure of the sediment in his mouthful of brew, the farmer announced "There, you had one of the rough, now we'll go in and have one of the smooth," and then ushered him on into the house for a glass of whiskey.

There was a good deal for an itinerant musician to absorb along with the fibrous red ale and the smooth Scotch: the depth of joy taken in the music, the embrace of celebratory tradition, and the love of the dance. Dudley was drawn to the feel of the English countryside. Even in the towns, the pathway to the pub wound its way through a field, by a stream, and perhaps inside a copse. He was touched by the friendliness of the people, and he has gone back to visit Bampton on two occasions.

In these traditional gatherings, inseparable from the places they sprang up in thousands of years ago, Dudley encountered physical evidence of the tidal pull of ancient celebration that he had felt intuitively drawn to for years. Since about 1947, he had been acting on a sense of personal calling, creative energy, and cultural responsibility for the body of a three-hundred-year-old tradition of New England contradance. At one time, like so much of the founding American ethic, that legacy had seemed ticketed for extinction. It must have been something of a revelation to go over the water and experience rural folk dance culture that could actually be carbon-traced through a set of reindeer antlers to the year *before* the Battle of Hastings. After taking her turn at wielding the horns, young English folksinger Rachel Unthank could say, emphatically: "This tradition has never been revived. It's continuous, it goes back hundreds of years in generations of families. They bend the rules to fit time and circumstances but they don't feel threatened that it might dilute their tradition since there's an inner confidence that is unquestionable."[121] It is evidently all pagan with a "small p" and

---

121. Abbots Bromley Horn Dance video by Roddy Melville, accessed on YouTube.

resurrection with a "capital R" on the walls of St. Nicholas Church in old Abbots Bromley.

"Keeping the faith" in community seemed to be easier to do when people set aside time to repeat the Apostle's creeds of tradition through holiday and celebration. The old ways of rural England and their surviving cousins in countrysides all around the globe provide a reminder of the basic collaborative and celebratory elements of human nature. Before rural people became gelded by modern fashion, they took much of the measure of their vigorous lives in ritual and holiday. Not a month went by without some generative and instinctual community marking of season and circumstance. In the darkest and coldest days of the year, they simply knocked off for about a month and celebrated good food, family, fine fellowship, old stories, and tunes known "by heart."[122] As the young year progressed, they gathered together to celebrate the sweets of May, to speed the plow, to haste to the wedding, to fill the basket, to move to the fair, and then, as the days shortened, to give good gifts, one to another. Before they knew it, they'd all come 'round right to the season of figgy puddings and boughs of holly. With moods and spirits fit for all seasons, the people could freely and truly rejoice in who and in where they were.

Characteristically, Dudley took it upon himself to import, graft, transplant, or improvise Old-World seasonal celebration in music in the forests and meadows of his hometown of Canterbury. Under his tutelage, a New Year's tradition called "The Ride" began to be observed in the 1970s. Early in the winter, under the moniker of "Dudley Laufman, Dance Caller, Musician, Poet," he would send out an invitation/reminder/summons to his vast mailing list, putting them on notice as in this manner:

> *For thirty years or more Canterbury musicians,*
> *singers, and dancers have visited homes in the area*
> *on New Year's Day. (For a few years we did the tour*

---

122. A phrase worth pondering.

on Halloween, the first day of winter.) The arrival at each home is usually noisy, snow on boots. We play a few chunes, sing a wassail, do a wintertime Morris dance, do a mummers play, then get the company up to do the dreaded ribbon dance and a few others. Sing a last song, then we are plied with nut brown ale and goodies before traveling on to the next place. For the first time, my place here on Shaker Road, Wind In the Timothy, is going to be the last stop. Other hosts usually invite friends, neighbors, relatives. As most of the Riders are my friends and neighbors, I would like to invite a few folks who are outside this circle. Keep in mind this is not a contra dance, but there will be some dancing. Please leave your car at the road, thanks. Please bring some food to share, and some drink. I will have some food and ale here. If you get here and nobody is here, it means we are still carrying on at Steve Fifields. Just come in and make yourself to home. We will arrive soon.

We party this way every year, to welcome back the sun as the days start getting longer. We call it The Ride after the Cajuns on Mardi Gras in Louisiana, traditionally ride from farm to farm on horseback, picking up the makings for a big gumbo. They have a glass and a few chunes at each place, arriving eventually at the big house to make the gumbo and dance. They ride on horseback. We ride in cars, but we Ride."[123]

This event took a leading place in a calendar of Canterbury country events that picked up again at the annual sugaring off party in March at Roy Hutchinson's, where Dudley played to the accompaniment of crackling pine and steaming syrup and where

---

123. E-mail from Dudley Laufman, 12/17/19.

the hard cider flowed like the snowmelt in the little brook outside. Summer saw a Sweets of May celebration, followed later on by the annual Canterbury Fair, which combined traditional country crafts and displays with improvised forms of rural jollification.[124] Dudley convened a collection of like-minded antiquarians and fostered the introduction of Morris dancing to the old Shaker town. The winter solstice in Canterbury is marked by ritual and song. In many of these events, Dudley played the part of player-coach, a role to which he was uniquely suited.

It was no wonder that in New England, folk would convene on holiday and holy day, fiddling during maple sugaring parties, quaffing the Guinness on St. Patrick's Day, plank-dancing at a Pinkster festival,[125] walking in reverential procession through the North End behind the statue of a Madonna, winding through the streets of Chinatown alongside a huge dragon, showing cattle at the county fair, and, in the waning light of November, gathering together to feast on turkeys, cranberries, and the sweet corn and pumpkins that the ancient ones had been harvesting for thousands of years. All the meanwhile came the Monday night contras in Nelson, the Friday night squares in Porter Square, and the shindigs up at places like the Blue Goose in Northport, Maine, worth the long ride for the music in the hall and the seafood platters that could be found nearby in Belfast.

Like the bloom of cardinal flowers and the call of whip-poor-wills, dances, fairs, and old home days come back year after year and remind us who we are and what we're doing here in New England. In the era of machines, we have become adept at breaking our own hearts, and in much too much of a hurry to "pick up the pieces of

---

124. Not long after the Bicentennial of 1976, an impromptu "hippies vs. rednecks" log-rolling contest was held in the little town pond, an event that the participants may not have yet completely recovered from.

125. The African-American folk celebration of the eighteenth and nineteenth centuries that served as one of the major blending points of European and African cultures in America.

pain" that we have inflicted, upon ourselves as much as on anyone. The damage done by "progress in our time" has gone far, far beyond the realm of collateral. Yet there is a wealth of healing to be found in traditional music, in tunes that hold the measure of time and tides, of loves and losses, and in songs that seek to gather us all together, once and ever again, in safety and in benediction.

⧉15⧉

Honors, Recordings, Reunions,
and a Living Legacy

THE YEAR 2006 saw Dudley produce two new CD recordings at the age of seventy-six. The first, titled *Where'd You Get Them Great Chunes?*[126] was a collection of a dozen reels, hornpipes, and a jig, all played and called by Dudley, with Ken Siegal and with the Sugar River Band, composed of Jane Orzechowski, Francis Orzechowski, Sophie Orzechowski, and Neil Orzechowski. The collection was well-received, and was soon followed by a solo anthology of seventeen songs, tunes, and stories by Dudley that was titled, simply, *Chocolate Soda.* The engaging release presents a compilation of his talents, his experiences, and his boyhood exploits in the streets of the old dowager town of Boston.

The course of time brought increased awareness of Dudley Laufman's role in the revival of traditional dance throughout in New England and beyond. In 2001, he was awarded the New Hampshire Governor's Arts Award in Folk Heritage. In 2009, Dudley was chosen to receive the National Heritage Fellowship from the National Endowment for the Arts, the United States government's highest honor in the folk and traditional arts. He joined more than 270 past

---

126. The title lifted from Dudley's English friend Johnny Wipple's response to hearing *Mistwold,* years before.

honorees, including such national treasures as Bill Monroe, Sonny Terry, Brownie McGee, Sister Mildred Barker, Almeda Riddle, Elizabeth Cotton, Ralph Stanley, Doc Watson, Earl Scruggs, B. B. King, Pops Staples, Bob McQuillen, Jean Ritchie, Mavis Staples, and Mike Seeger. This was tall cotton, particularly as product of the short growing season of New Hampshire. His citation read:

> *The name Dudley Laufman is so closely associated with the contra and barn dances of New England that most long-term residents refer to local gatherings as "Dudley Dances." Two forms of community dances evolved in New England—contra dances, done in lines with partners facing one another, and square dances featuring sets of four couples. After the Revolutionary War, dances such as these, associated with England, fell out of favor, except in the rural areas of the Northeast where they continued to occur in informal settings such as kitchen parties and barn dances. Laufman came to New Hampshire in 1947 to work at a dairy farm and began to attend these local dances. He called his first dance in 1948 and soon started his own musical group for the dances, which later became the Canterbury Country Dance Orchestra. During the 1970s, the orchestra made a number of recordings, and Laufman traveled throughout the region, performing and teaching dance at schools, community centers, and public parks, averaging 300 or more engagements each year…Ernest Thompson, New Hampshire resident and author of On Golden Pond, succinctly conveys Laufman's contributions to New England dance: "I think Dudley Laufman belongs in the pantheon of genuine American artists. He belongs in Franconia Notch, the real Old Man of the Mountain."*

Jacqueline and Dudley traveled to Washington to receive the honor. The master of ceremonies made the introduction by saying

"When you speak about dance in New England there's a name that comes to mind…Dudley Laufman…He has been making this kind of music, calling the dances for more than 40 years, please welcome him to the stage…" Applause followed, then Neil Orzechowski began playing the tune "Mistwold" on piano, joined by Sylvia Miskoe on accordion, and Jacqueline Laufman, Ted Levin, Vince O'Donnell and Dudley on fiddles. A lively group of dancers followed Dudley's calling, including, as Dudley announced: "My daughter Heidi, my son Nathaniel, my sister Ann, her daughter Sarah, my grandson Max, my daughter Wendy, Jacqueline's daughter Laura, my grandson Jacob, my daughter Bronwen, and my daughter Singwen." He then turned to his partner and announced "I wouldn't have got this award without Jacqueline!" The audience, full of New Hampshire folk who had made the trip down, applauded, and, after the ceremonies, gathered in private celebration. It was a night long to remember.[127]

Dudley Laufman has been fortunate to inspire extraordinary collaboration throughout his career, and beginning around 2014 an informal confluence of enthusiastic souls convened to help define and preserve his legacy and that of the Canterbury Country Dance Orchestra. Jacqueline Laufman, Jack Sloanaker, Gerry Putnam of Cedarhouse Sound and Mastering, and a volunteer from Folk New England joined forces to locate, restore, digitize, catalogue, and archive as many of his original reels of tapes as could be found. By and large, most were in relatively good shape after more than thirty years in storage. Their restoration involved a considerable amount of hard work and expense, but the effort was well worth it "for the love of the music."

Early in 2016, Jacqueline Laufman sought to convene a reunion of the Canterbury Country Dance Orchestra. She enlisted a total of sixteen musicians, circulated sheet music of tunes chosen by Dudley, made arrangements with the Middlesex School for use of the chapel,

---

127. The year 2007 also saw the release of *The Other Way Back*, a well-received video documentary by David Millstone that presents an overview of Dudley's work and its national impact.

and worked tirelessly with Gerry Putnam of Cedarhouse Sound to organize the single day recording session held on March 16, 2016. Gerry played the multiple roles of producer, recorder, and engineer in the course of the day-long session. He began by "reading" the sound dynamics of the spacious hall, positioned the microphones for optimum coverage, and achieved the desired balance by moving the musicians around as needed. There was a quick practice run-through before each take, all of which went flawlessly. Putnam signaled "recording" as he set the tapes rolling and the musicians fell into the tunes. As each number approached its close, Greg Boardman stood up and signaled the final notes with a nod of his head and a flourish of his fiddle bow, and then after a few buffering seconds of silence, Gerry Putnam announced the end of the take. "I loved doing it the old-fashioned way," he remembers. "It was a majestic day!"

This *Welcome Here Again*[128] project was an artistic *tour de force* timed towards the latter stages of a number of distinguished careers and at the promising beginnings of others. The group of assembled musicians included Sylvia Miskoe playing accordion, Art Bryan on the ringing banjo, and Vince O'Donnell on fiddle, all stalwart Canterbury members from the 1960s. Jack Perron played fiddle, Allen McIntyre the concertina, Carl Jacobs the bass, Wally Sweet the flute, Jane Orzechowski and Greg Boardman the fiddle, and Taylor Whiteside guitar; all musicians from somewhat later points in the life of the orchestra. Youthful players Sophie Orzechowski and Neil Orzechowski, on fiddle, Russell Orzechowski on piano, and Jordan Tyrell-Wysocki on fiddle completed the roster, with Jacqueline Laufman playing fiddle and Dudley presiding on accordion and on harmonica throughout. It was the fourth album that a large Canterbury Country Dance Orchestra group recorded at the scene of some of its greatest accomplishments, and it more than lived up to the excellence of its predecessors.

Dudley's choice of material was key; in many ways the playlist shared the sense of soaring gravitas that had come across

---

128. *Welcome Here Again,* Canterbury Country Dance Orchestra, 2016.

so consistently in the group's first album in 1971. "Sweet Richard" was one example of this "feel," ancient and stately yet sprightly, and played with striding, celebratory confidence. Russell Orzechowski's piano cadence anchors the piece, perhaps at a bit more of a Lipizzaner pace than Bob McQuillen's Clydesdale stride, but nonetheless in the same tradition. A dynamic balance was struck between young and old in the artists; their common denominators were excellence and inspiration. The one contemporary "outlier" in the repertoire of venerable tunes was Jordan Tyrell-Wysocki's composition "Charley Murray's Waltz" which is one of the most moving performances in the group's half-century body of work. The project aimed high and, to the credit of all of its guardian angels, it exceeded its lofty goals.[129] Dudley's long and fruitful partnership with Jacqueline Laufman came to an end later in 2016.

On July 15, 2012, scores of friends had gathered at the Peterborough Unitarian Church to honor Bob McQuillen. "We are all together, all part of the music," noted Gordon Peery in his fine opening remarks. After a program presented by Bob on piano and his musical partners Jane Orzechowski on fiddle and Deanna Stiles on flute, scores of musicians walked into the church in procession (with Vince O'Donnell in the van and Dudley bringing up the rear) to join in honoring Bob with a beautiful rendition of his tune "Amelia." Bob passed away at age ninety on February 9, 2014. Renn Tolman, Frank Upton, and Barney Quigley had been among the last survivors of the old Nelson crowd; Frank passed on in 2006, Renn in 2014, and Barney in 2016. Around that time, at an outdoor concert one night in West Brattleboro, Vermont, Art Bryan had the fascinating experience of congratulating a young banjo player on his music, and having the kid say "I've been inspired by the records of an old guy named Art Bryan. I never got to meet him, and I imagine he's dead now." Art assured the youthful banjo picker that such was not the case.

---

129. The recording of *Welcome Here Again* and John Gfroerer's production in 2016 were made possible through the generosity of private lovers of the music through a grant from Folk New England, Inc.

There had never been a complete CD collection put together of Dudley's musical compositions, and in 2019 fiddler Lindsay Holden initiated a creative recording project that would respond to that need. Twenty tunes were chosen, and ten musicians invited to convene on the bright morning of April 7, 2019, out on Shaker Road in the house Dudley built of used lumber in 1957. Donuts and coffee were served, the bird feeder was filled, and the group dove into the music. Sylvia Miskoe played accordion, Art Bryan the banjo, and Dudley the melodion; Jane Orzechowski, Lindsay Holden, Greg Boardman, and Russell Orzechowski comprised the fiddle section; Sue Hunt keyed the piano; Walt Sweet played the flute; Bill Zecker manned the bass, and Tom Curren played guitar in this latest incarnation of the Canterbury Country Dance Orchestra. Gerry Putnam of Cedarhouse Studios presided over the recording, which went perfectly, with only two re-takes required. It may not have been an Easter Sunday, yet it felt like one.

By virtue of their written lyrics, two of the compositions ("Mistwold" and "Glenn Towle") qualified as "songs" as well as "tunes." About a month after the session on Shaker Road, Dudley, Lindsay Holden, Gerry Putnam, and Tom Curren gathered at Cedarhouse Studios to record a vocal track, with Dudley singing the lyrics and the rest of the crew joining in on the choruses. On the recording master, Gerry Putnam patched the vocal rendition into the beginning of each of those cuts, followed a beat or two later by the instrumental recorded back in Canterbury. The CD graphics were designed by Lindsay Holden, and included a booklet of Dudley's stories about tunes, old friends, cardinal flowers, and whip-poor-will songs. *Here's To Every Country Dancer*[130] took its place in the long collection of Canterbury recordings, and bore witness to the music and the musicians and dancers that kept the faith with it.

Less than a year after the recording of *Here's To Every Country Dancer*, the pandemic outbreak of 2020 put a prudential close to most public gatherings. Contradances were canceled, the traditional

---

130. *Here's To Every Country Dancer*, Canterbury Country Dance Orchestra, 2019.

New Year's afternoon musical Canterbury "Ride" shrank in size, and even the annual sugaring off party at Roy Hutchinson's "Sap 'n Cida" maple sugar house was put aside, with the 2019 crop of hard cider left to ripen for the duration. Dudley contracted Covid and got through it in one piece at the age of ninety. Under the circumstances, little could be predicted in the public realm, and we all await better days when the community gathering of country dance becomes a matter of safe routine once again. We keep the faith.[131] It does seem clear, though, that whenever and wherever people gather to play and to dance, there will be a good mix of old timers and capable new players like Sophie Orzechowski, Neil Orzechowski, Russell Orzechowski, Jordan Tyrell-Wysocki, and Art Bryan's young banjo protégé in line to carry on the traditions that Dudley, Bob McQuillen, and many others had fostered in them and in thousands of good people over the decades and on all sides of all the ponds.[132]

The vital but fragile joy of contradance that Dudley Laufman discovered as a youth has become a thriving art form throughout the country, due in large part to his stewardship and dedication. He points to the Maine Country Dance Orchestra and the Lamprey River Band in New Hampshire as extensions of his work; scores of other music groups around the country would also cite the force of his influence and his inspiration. Prominent among these is a vital volunteer traditional music community from Massachusetts that calls itself "Roaring Jelly," whose life and times are described for us by one of its members:

> *In 1970, a number of people started gathering*
> *informally to play folk music at Ann Gary's house*

---

131. On May 19, 2022, Dudley reported to me that he'd dreamt that he'd gotten a grant to do a special event on early New Hampshire dancing.

132. In 2020, the New Hampshire State Council on the Arts put out a brochure titled "Live Free and Dance," that listed a "traditional dance trail" that included whistle stops in Concord, Boscawen, Canterbury, Durham, East Derry, Kingston, Londonderry, Milford, Nelson, Norwich (Vermont), Peterborough, Tamworth, and near the Seacoast in Newfields.

in Wayland, Massachusetts. Dan and Molly Watt participated in these sessions, and, along with their daughters, attended Folk Music Week at Pinewoods Camp in 1972, where Dudley Laufman called dances every night. They loved the dancing, and Dudley told them that they should be going to Dance Week instead. That experience led to the band organizing a dance in the Town Hall in Lincoln, Massachusetts, and later on, at a stone church nearby which had the benefit of a sturdier dance floor. Once a week, the musicians convened to practice, and each dance commenced when the number of dancers exceeded the number of musicians in attendance. The dances provided a place for many callers and musicians to try out teaching and playing, a number of whom went on to call and play extensively for dancing, both locally and throughout the country. The dances later moved to Arlington and then to Lexington, where they have continued to take place until the pandemic. Band members continue to rehearse twice a month and eagerly await the return to playing for dancers. The group counts over 350 enthusiastic and loyal alums at present.

Stalwart member Vince O'Donnell remembers: "In the summer of '72, Dudley told me about this group of people that were practicing in Wayland…a good way to get to know people and a good way to build a repertoire." It was begun as having as its basic value "an ensemble you can join in with when you're not all that good!" A combination of camaraderie, humor, and joyful energy has stood its musicians and its community throughout Middlesex County in good stead for more than a half century. One of the Roaring Jelly musicians recalls being pulled over by a policeman for speeding on Route 2 west of Boston. When asked why she was exceeding the limit, she answered that she was part of the contradance group, that she was on her way back from a dance at the Town Hall, and that she must have been driving while humming along to a fast tune. The officer returned her license and registration to her without giving her a ticket, but with the admonition: "Next time, hum a waltz."[133]

Dudley has been appreciative of the accumulation of honors that have come his way, and rejoices in the fellowship of the musicians, dancers, and the lovers of tradition who have continued to gather together around country dance. He is more than a bit bemused by the degree of left-brain analysis that at times tends to be deployed to dissect, quantify, and categorize his work. "It's *music,* for God's sake!" And so it is, with all of its spontaneity, creativity, and joy. It seems worth remembering, particularly for a music archivist, that the nature of a butterfly is to move freely from milkweed flower to squash blossom and not to be pinned in a display case.

A fitting close to the chapter here might be a hand-written note left some years ago in the Nelson Town Hall by an experienced professional piano tuner who had been called in to service the town's old upright:

> *Because of the age of this piano and long abandoned construction practices, it is impossible to give this piano a highly accurate tuning. It has numerous false beats, in harmonicity, and heavy wear. Surprisingly, the overall tone is superior and the action is still fast and responsive. I suspect the piano is favored by those who play on it.*

---

133. Special thanks to Debby Knight, who supplies us with this delightful account. Roaring Jelly's wonderful fiftieth anniversary video can be found on the New England Folk Festival website at neffa.org. Under 2022 Festival Community videos, select the first choice (Roaring Jelly Turns 50). The engaging piece features a black-and-white film fragment of a 1960s dance in Richmond, NH, with Dudley, Sylvia Miskoe, Joe Ryan, and Nicholas Howe playing for an enthusiastic group of dancers.

═ 16 ═

The Wind in the Timothy

A T ABOUT THE SAME TIME in 1971 that Dudley Laufman was convening the musicians who would create "The Blue Album," Professor Charles E. Clark of the University of New Hampshire was taking to the podium at Bates College in Maine to deliver an address on the history of northern New England.[134] Clark's talk was a multi-faceted gem that is well-worth seeking out. The former newspaper editor covered hundreds of years of time and space with as much craft, verve, and subtlety as Dudley and his crew were deploying in the music at the Middlesex School Chapel.

As he explored his subject, Charles Clark observed that the defining regional art form hereabouts is the development of individual personality. In his theory, before anyone in New England could go forth to become a competent farmer, librarian, town cop, or storekeeper, they would need to discover, develop, perfect, *and learn how to express* a unique personality. Following this line of reasoning, then, it becomes clear that the basic job of any Yankee woman or man is to become "a piece of work."

---

134. Charles E. Clark, "Beyond The Frontier: An Environmental Approach to The Early History of Northern New England" in *Maine Historical Society Newsletter*, Vol. 11 No. 1 (Portland: Maine Historical Society, 1971), 5–21.

The more one thinks about this, the more it rings true, or at least it explains a lot. Human existence is a tough row to hoe. Civilization is a fine idea in theory, but it remains very much a work in progress, one that is often observed, at least historically, in the breach as much as it is in the performance. The modern temptation to enter into misguided beliefs and engage in expedient but ill-advised behaviors is overwhelming. Cynicism and social conformity predispose us to misadventure, right up until we begin to take notice that our ears have begun to grow pointed and sprout fuzz, as if we were members of the wayward gang of boys in the old story of *Pinocchio*.

It is a comfort to our most cherished regional prejudices to think that New Englanders have figured out a serviceable way to proceed in the face of our rigorous prevailing winds and across the course of our frost-heaved footing. We need look no further than the local postmistress, hardware store owner, contractor, or dump-keeper to find souls who manage to turn the course of their days into sort of a sonnet, and maybe even into an act in a long-running improvisational play. A whole lot of folks learn to go about their business speaking in personalized free verse, the kind that you find yourself replaying when you drive out of the lumberyard after a conversation with someone who is all dusted over with old stories and sawdust. It's not a bad way to get through the day, and it's also not a bad way to maintain a caring relationship with your neighbors without actually having to display affection. The heart of the matter is to turn your daily business into the sort of interactive art that feels good, wears well, grows on folks, and that can actually be a lot of fun.

Yet turning your personality into a work of art is a lot easier than it is to turn your art into a business. There are often very few advantages that an artist has access to in America; the muse here is almost always swimming against the tide. In New England, the artistic gauntlet is encumbered with random moorings, stray gill nets, and bobbing lobster pots, since everything is pretty much defined, these days, by its capacity to turn a bit of coin. Distracted by shiny objects, the Yankee artist is always in danger of fetching up on a half-tide ledge, or at the very least, getting tangled up in rockweed.

No wonder at all that a creative soul like Emily Dickinson would choose to stay on dry land and cultivate her art in private, as if her poems were a collection of African violets best tucked away neatly on the shelves of a quiet conservatory.

In order to successfully express the New England character, an artist needs to discover how to seize moment, medium, and mission firmly and publicly. Harriet Beecher Stowe did this in the service of the national conscience. Robert Frost figured out how to do it in verse, insight, and attitude, and Julia Child blended ingredients of food and personality to great effect. Our old neighbor Don Hall skillfully grafted poetry, prose, and public speaking together. On the baseball diamond, David Ortiz mastered the moment with a waning summer on the line and a whole region's hopes held in his heart and hands.

Among other New England experts at self-definition were the Wabanaki women of the Laurent family who, years ago, used to sell sweetgrass baskets to summer folks by the side of Route 16 in the village of Intervale, New Hampshire. In August, on the way back from Pinkham Notch, my mom would instruct my dad to pull the station wagon over so that she could visit with the Native craftswomen, listen to their stories, and buy Christmas presents from them. Mom was drawn to do the things in daily life that she felt would bring her closer to God; remembering the look on her face as our big Ford and its assorted cargo headed south towards Sanbornville, I think this was one of them.

To any roster of Yankee poets, reformers, sluggers, novelists, and craftspeople, we can add the names of square dance callers like Happy Hale, Arthur Hanson, Ralph Page, and all the dance prompters and musicians worth their salt who ever filled a floor and kept it hopping between Quebec and Connecticut. It is easy to recognize the value of the work of all these people, as well as the pivotal role played by Dudley Laufman in the conservation and cultivation of this collective folk tradition. As Vince O'Donnell has noted, "Dudley was the leading edge at a certain point in time. He brought people into the community even as he developed a visceral approach to tradition. He excelled at achieving a nuance in the sound that results in respect being shown to the music. He accomplished this by his attitude and by his example...there's no book for learning that." Everyone from the threshold of Roy Hutchinson's maple sugar house to the steps of the Smithsonian Institution has acknowledged his legacy. Ralph Page kept the traditions alive through the first half of the twentieth century and Dudley Laufman has seen them through the perils, delusions, and attention-deficits of the following seventy years through his dedication, his force of will, his charisma, and his love of the music. His is a hugely important body of life's work.

As of this writing, contradances are said to be held regularly in about ninety locations in New England. Just under sixty persons list themselves as callers, and something in the neighborhood of a hundred bands are in business in the field of traditional dance music.[135] These are almost certainly undercounts, but they indicate clearly the renewed vitality of the tradition and speak well of its prospects for the future. The revival of country dance in New England should be seen as the collective accomplishment of dozens of gifted musicians, many of whom came into the creative orbit of the Canterbury Country Dance Orchestra. Bob McQuillen began by playing the accordion for Ralph Page, and his piano anchored the Canterbury sound for decades. His low-key personal style provided something of a counterbalance to Dudley's charismatic presence. Like Dudley, Bob mentored dozens of gifted musicians during his long lifetime, and his *Great Meadow Collection* legacy includes more than 1,300 tunes of his composition.

Newt Tolman's *Nelson Music Collection,* written in 1969 with Kay Gilbert, was re-released in 2013 with a new foreword by his son, Renn. Sylvia Miskoe was awarded the Governor's New Hampshire Folk Heritage Award in 2011 "for her deep and long-lasting influence on New Hampshire's traditional music and dance and... her contributions to our state's musical lore." Rodney Miller's career as fiddler, fiddle-maker, composer, author, and general past-keeper

---

135. http://www.contradancelinks.com/newengland.html. Produced by Charlie Seelig.

has spanned decades. In 1983, he was designated a Master Fiddler by the National Endowment for the Arts.

Art Bryan joined forces with his wife, Laurie, Sarah Bauhan, and Jane Orzechowski in their band called Strathspey, recording cuts on the *New England Contradance* CD on Kicking Mule Records. Earning a distinction that can only be termed "historic," the members of the group were the first musicians to play at the Press Room in Portsmouth, New Hampshire.[136] Art documented scores of beautiful old tunes for posterity in the recorded collection of 108 traditional numbers that he compiled in partnership with George Fowler and others titled *The Montville Project*. Vince O'Donnell's long musical career is only a portion of his growing legacy; his work in fair housing and social justice brought him recognition by the National Housing and Rehabilitation Association in 2013.

In 2021, Randy Miller was awarded the New Hampshire Governor's Folk Heritage Award. His citation included an account of his impact on the field of traditional dance music, citing *The New England Fiddler's Repertoire*, first published in 1983 and revised and reissued twenty-five years later, and other tune collections—*Irish Traditional Fiddle Music*, in collaboration with Jack Perron, and *The Fiddler's Throne*—that have recorded, with amazing fidelity, "the rich heritage of Irish and American fiddle music in New England." Greg Boardman has been a leading figure in traditional music in Maine for years, as founder of the Maine Fiddle Camp and as the teacher of hundreds of young instrumentalists. The folks on the extended Canterbury roster were more than outstanding musicians. Many are remarkable souls who continue to make deep and sustaining impressions on their colleagues and in their communities.

Ted Levin played on the first three recordings of the Canterbury Country Dance Orchestra before embarking upon a career in ethnomusicology that brought him to engage in pioneering work in Central Asia, to earn a doctorate from Princeton, to become the

---

136. Possibly as early as 1976, launching a tradition in that storied Portsmouth watering hole.

chair of the Music Department at Dartmouth College, and to play a leading role in the 2002 Smithsonian Folklife Festival devoted to the Silk Road. Ted has authored several books on Central Asian music and became an authority on the subject through a combination of fieldwork, relationships, study, and advocacy. He has acted as both a scholar and a culture broker in places where intact examples still remain of some of humanity's oldest musical traditions.

At Dartmouth College on February 28, 2012, Ted presented the annual Faculty Presidential Lecture entitled "Why Music Matters," which he concluded with the following words: "In the end, what I most cherish, both about making music and listening to it in live performance, is the mysterious advent, sometimes in a moment of repose, and sometimes in a moment of heightened attention, of a frisson, a chill, or a sudden welling up of tears that is the physical manifestation of awe, wonder, or exhilaration. Such responses, whatever the musical language that delivers them, are a birthright of all humans; indeed, responding to music humanizes us, and reaffirms why music matters." For decades, his work and that of his fellow Canterbury musicians has served to meet that standard.[137]

Like the women weaving baskets by the side of the road, like a good dairy farmer with dung fork in hand, like the lady who makes quilts for the League of New Hampshire Crafts Fair that look like a blanket of autumn leaves, the work of past-keeping is all about the faithful repetition of inherited inspiration. It's about a lifetime of listening to your heart instead of the guidance counselors, of paying attention to the good stuff that everyone else is ignoring, of figuring out the chords and the recipes, practicing the stitches and the carvings, making the phone calls, lining up the hall, buying the lumber, remembering to bring the donuts. Sometimes it's about unpaid bills and broken

---

137. Theodore Levin, Arthur R. Virgin Professor of Music at Dartmouth College, presented the annual faculty Presidential Lecture on Tuesday, February 28, 2012. His lecture, entitled "Why Music Matters," is available on YouTube.

hearts and trucks that won't pass inspection in February, and, after they do, that get bogged down in a mud hole in March. Sometimes you do things you wish you hadn't, or at least you might figure out, later, that you could have done differently. Sometimes you have to walk all the way back from Concord to Canterbury after sundown, carrying your accordion in a backpack after collecting your pay in the form of a few worn dollar bills. Sometimes it starts to snow in the dark and you don't know it till the flakes begin to melt on your forehead.

Books like this are supposed to deliver the reader safely to a handy moral bus-stop, but we'll settle for a few suggestions here, if that's all right with you. One would be to encourage you to go to a contradance which, as fiddler Donna Hebert says, is the most fun you can have with your clothes on. There is much more nourishment to be found in live music than there is in prying open a can of the processed kind. Fortunately, you can still find ample sources of fresh, organic music in New England; sometimes right under the same roof with the good local food in a farmer's market. You might seek to find out the time of the next contradance, sugaring off party, Old Home Day, or the seasonal opening of a farm stand, and circle the calendar as if that date was as transformative as the readjustment of the clocks in the spring and the fall. When you get inside the Grange hall and your glasses un-fog, don't just stare or paw over the musician's CDs, the author's books, or the farmer's dozen eggs or honey jars on the fold-up table. *Act like a piece of work,* for goodness sake, just as your ancestors did. Pull your wallet out of your pocket and do your part in creative commerce between real, living human beings for a change. That *will* be a change, of the kind that we can all get to keep.

The renewed popularity of contradance in the 1960s coincided with a period of deep division and crisis in American life. Young people discovered that traditional music could act as a saving grace as they tried to traverse in safety and harmony across a troubled landscape.

Back in 1937, Ralph Page had suggested that a revival of country dance could be the "first crocus in the recovery of civilization from its self-poisoning." We have more than good and sufficient reason to recall his words since we have learned that so much of what glitters at us these days is proving to be toxic as well as specious. After stumbling through the snowdrifts of a long winter of discontent, any emerging blooms of truth and beauty will well be worth our gratitude and our care. By cultivating an abiding faith in a generative future, we can muster the fortitude and the skills that will enable it to happen. Should we choose to do so, we can engage in the process of calling our own tunes and dancing together to them, once again.

Vitality, optimism, creativity, and the physical manifestation of craft seem to be among the common ingredients of folk culture that await our rediscovery. In the case of country dances, these may simply have been the components of a healthy society that felt free, and perhaps even felt compelled, to express the joy and vigor of human nature in tunes and in steps. The ancient composers drew a body of work forth from their lives that still remains capable of illuminating the present day. They were as anonymous, as dedicated, and as inspired as the craftspeople who fashioned the rose windows in the cathedrals of France around the same time. The tradition of community music that they left behind has served as a defining force in all the summers of our dreams, in the towns that know us well, and in the region that will always take us in when we have no place to go. Over the long centuries, creative commonality has integrated people's lives with those of their neighbors. Nowadays, we're not so sure about ourselves, and so it gets hard for us to be sure of one another. It need not be so.

As we have learned to work "remotely," we have been called to remember things in family and nearby fellowship that can no longer be trusted to the calculation of distant experts. We are coming to the realization that there is good reason to reform a modern culture that wants to indenture us to algorithm, to mortgage us to convention, and that tries to beguile us into thinking that convenience is a good reason to overdraw the inherited natural accounts that support our very lives.

The living world is always full of yeasty possibilities. Some choices, perhaps many of them, are more generative, or at least a lot more fun, than the ones that we have been accustomed to making of late. We may be arriving at a good time to consider a novel and a radical application of our oldest common traditions. In craft, in music, in art, and in writing, we are called again to hear our ancestor's voices, to hearken to the antique tunes, to dance once more to the echoes of ancient instruments good and true.

The accrued magic in old music is always there for us to embrace. Sometimes the tunes are simple and sturdy, like the posts and the carrying beams of the Nelson Town Hall. Sometimes the notes soar skyward like the steeple of the North Church in Portsmouth, in the sort of benediction that marks our places in the churchyard, by the altar, and in the baptismal font. Chord the melodion, key the piano, rosin up the bow, and release yourself in the wild flight of the flute. Honor your partner, bow to your corner, let us all hold hands now. Way, hey, and away we go in the promenade back home, back to the place where we can recall all the old stories and we can remember, once again, who it is that we are and who we want ourselves to be.

Two Poems and a Piece
by Dudley Laufman

The Sweets of May

The spice of the currant blossom
Floats upon the air.
Makes my feet go up and down,
A garland in my hair.

For I am a country dancer.
The best you've ever seen.
Golden is my partner
With a smock of green.

We dance around the lilacs
And through the greeny grass
As the music slides and trembles
And the May lasts

On into the summer,
June and then July,
Autumn and longy winter
All the seasons die.

O how I miss the springtime
And the May again,
When the men dance round the ladies
And the ladies go round the men

How Contra Dancing Was Invented

Started off as a cash crop. Had to entertain them summerfolk on Saturday nights. Got Uncle Walter to show us the figures 'n steps to them old contry's and quadrilles. We called 'em square dances. Hollis & Quint played their flute & fiddle. They'd get Arno on his guitar, and go down to that abandoned cider mill, had that brook running underneath it, smell of pomace and rotting wood. Sit there in the lantern light, pass a bottle around, play the old dance tunes with that great echo.

Uncle Walter's nephew would sit in a dark corner. Couldn't see him, quiet feller. Surprised everyone by lilting out in his flute-fiddle voice, chanting his changes to Hull's Victory, like he'd been doing it all his life. He was a natural. They pressed him into service at the very next dance.

You know how the story goes from here. How the hippies came to the dances with their patchouli oil and bare feet, how they didn't like the word "square," and how they discovered some were contras. We heard one of them tell someone "It's not square dancing, it's contra dancing. It's not square dancing, it's contra dancing."

The rest is history except some of us old folks up here who still like to say we're going to the square dance.

Fiddle Camps

Fiddlers Mellie Dunham and George Overlock,
Mainers of the first hair, had about thirty tunes
in their repertoire: Turkey In The Straw, Irish
Washerwoman, Soldier's Joy, Campbells Are Coming,
and like that, for contras Lady of the Lake, Boston
Fancy, Mountain Ranger, Haymakers. They swapped
those tunes around for those dances, to do the job.
Then someone, lord knows who, came across Cincinnati
Hornpipe and Top of Cork Road Jig, and dances that
went with them. More music was discovered, more
dances, more people to play them. New tunes and dances
written like McQuillen's Squeezebox, Nantucket
Sleighride, which made for an enormous surplus of music
and dances which then necessitated the advent of the use
of medleys, (three chunes or more per contra.) but even
so there was not enough days in the week for them to
play all the music for all the dances, so the need for fiddle
camps arose, followed by dance camps and organic
farms to feed them all, and now everyone is a fiddler,
dancer, farmer, or all of the above at once and nobody has
time to do anything else like go to war or shit like that.

Appendix

Selected recordings released by Dudley Laufman with the Canterbury Country Dance Orchestra and with Other Friends.

Canterbury Country Dance Orchestra ("The Blue Album")
Recorded at the Middlesex School Chapel, Concord, MA. Saturday, September, 25 1971, released spring 1972 as F&W Records FW-3
All tunes in the public domain.

1) Farewell To Whiskey/Money Musk	3:23	In A
2.) The Flight (Mutual Love)	2:53	In C
3.) Petronella	3:40	In D
4.) Kalendera Kola	1:17	
5.) Coleraine	3:24	
6.) Prince William	4:05	
7.) Irish American Reel	3:35	In F
8.) Chorus Jig	2:59	In D and G
9.) Huntsman's Chorus	3:17	

10.) Petronella (with calls)	1:21	In D
11.) Auretti's Dutch Skipper	3:26	
12.) Poor Auld Woman	3:09	
13.) Yarmouth Reel	3:31	In G
14.) Maguinnis' Delight	3:18	In F

Musicians: Allan Block, fiddle; Peter Colby, banjo and autoharp; Larry Delorier, flute, piccolo, and penny whistle; Dave Fuller, accordion; Nicholas S. Howe, fiddle; Dudley Laufman, accordion and calls; Ted Levin, fiddle; Bob McQuillen, piano and accordion; Jack Sloanaker, bass; Jerry Weene, fiddle and mandolin. Recorded by Seth Gibson. Audio tape restored and digitized by Gerry Putnam of Cedarhouse Studios, 7/4/17.

Excerpts from ***The Canterbury Orchestra Country Meets the F&W String Band*** ("The Orange Album")
Recorded at the Middlesex School Chapel, Concord, MA.
Saturday, September 23, 1972-released as F&W Records FW-4.
All tunes in public domain.

3.) Saddle the Pony	3:21
5.) Gentle Maiden	3:37
6.) Dorset Four Hand Reel	3:59
10.) Miss Dolland's Delight	3:32
11.) Larry O'Gaff	2:53
12.) Balkan Hills Schottische	4:15
14.) Meeting of the Waters	3:13

Canterbury Musicians: Fred Breunig, fiddle; Art Bryan, guitar; Peter Colby, autoharp and banjo; Larry Delorier, flute; Charlene Fagelman, flute; Dave Fuller, push box; Nicholas Howe, fiddle; Dudley Laufman, harmonica and fiddle; Ted Levin, fiddle, piano; Bob McQuillen, piano; Vince O'Donnell, fiddle and guitar; Jack Perron, fiddle; Jack Sloanaker, bass; Jerry Weene, viola, fiddle.

Dudley Laufman and Friends Live at the Coffin Factory
(unreleased tape)
Tape recorded at 88 Miller Street, Somerville, MA. Sunday, October 8, 1972.

1.) Marlboro Street (Dudley Laufman) 6:14 (Lady of the Lake contradance)

2.) Inga's Birthday (Dudley Laufman) 7:29 (Morning Star contradance)

3.) Miss Sayer's Allemande 4:58 (Miss Sayer's Allemande English country dance)

4.) Washington Quickstep 6:57 (Washington Quickstep contra)

5.) Chorus Jig 5:30 (Chorus Jig contradance)

6.) Star Label Reel 5:56 (Quadrille Dance)

7.) Madame Something 5:04 (Basket Quadrille Dance)

8.) Bonny Breastknot 6:56 (Bonny Breastknot contradance)

9.) Gaspe Reel 8:42 (Lady Bogart's Reel contra)

10.) DeMartelly (Dudley Laufman) 6:02 (DeMartelly contradance)

11.) Childgrove 7:15 (English contradance)

12.) Bobby Shafto/Simple Gifts 4:56 (French Four contradance)

Musicians: Dudley Laufman, accordion and calls; Fred Breunig, fiddle; Susan Champaney, harmonica; Jodi Evans, recorder; Charlene Fagelman, flute; David Langstaff, guitar and recorder; Randy Miller, guitar; Frank Perron, guitar; Jack Perron, fiddle, and Ken Siegal, fiddle. Recorded by Jack Sloanaker. Audio tape restored and digitized by Gerry Putnam of Cedarhouse Studios, Sutton, NH. 7/4/17

Itinerant Musicians License c.1973

33⅓ long-playing record, no label.

1.) Jenny's Gone To Linton	2:26	
2.) Bunch of Roses	2:58	
3.) Greensleeves	3:25	
4.) Constant Billy/ Bobbing Joe	2:51	
5.) Dressed Ship	2:40	
6.) Black Nag	1:18	
7.) Roxborough Castle	3:01	
8.) Lannigan's Ball	2:10	
9.) Queen's Jig	3:19	
10.) Kentish Cricketeers	2:51	
11.) Green Grow The Rushes/ Trip to Tunbridge	3:03	
12.) Pays de Haut	2:52	
13.) Flowers of the Thorn	3:00	
14.) Scollay's Reel	3:22	
15.) Balance The Straw	2:33	
16.) Swallow Tail Jig	2:54	
17.) Burley Ivy (Dudley Laufman)	2:18	
18.) Simple Gifts	3:36	(Coffin Factory 10/8/72)

Fred Breunig, Dudley Laufman, Randy Miller, and Jack Perron.

Mistwold

Canterbury Country Dance Orchestra

Recorded at the Middlesex School, Concord, MA.

F&W Records FW-5, 1974 All songs public domain except as noted.

51.9 minutes

1.) Mistwold (Dudley Laufman)	3:42
2.) A Starry Night To Ramble	3:53
3.) Colby's Medley (Peter Colby)	3:28

4.) Madame Bonaparte   4:45

5.) Balquidder Lasses   2:39

6.) Stornaway   2:54

7.) La Grondeuse   3:38

8.) Earl of Mansfield   3:39

9.) Madame Something-Or-Other   1:59

10.) Green Hills of Tyrol   3:02

11.) Prince William II   2:50

12.) Glenn Towle (Dudley Laufman)   5:29

13.) Madame Something   1:49   (from Coffin Factory
                                                       tape 10/8/72)

14.) Reel de Jeunne Marie   4:09

15.) Scottish Hornpipe   3:37

Musicians: Fred Breunig, fiddle; Art Bryan, guitar; Peter Colby, banjo, autoharp; Larry DeLorier, flute, piccolo, and penny whistle; Charlene Fagelman, flute; Dave Fuller, accordion; Nicholas Howe, fiddle; Dudley Laufman, accordion, harmonica, and fiddle; Ted Levin, fiddle, penny whistle; Bob McQuillen, piano, accordion; Vincent O'Donnell, fiddle, electric guitar; Jack Perron, fiddle; Jack Sloanaker, bass; Dick Van Cleek, French horn; Jerry Weene, fiddle.

CCDO Outtakes From 1971 And 1972

Three outtakes noted from *Canterbury Country Dance Orchestra* ("The Blue Album") include: Broken Lantern (in C); Planxty Denis O'Connor (in B flat), and Sprig of Shillelagh (also known as Black Joak). Also listed in early plans for the record were: Ah, Sure, Such a Pair (G), and Ned Kendall's Favorite Reel (D).

In addition to the cuts included on the *Mistwold* release, outtakes and alternate takes from the 1971 and 1972 recording sessions include the following titles, some in multiple versions: A Starry Night to Ramble; Madame Bonaparte; Finnegan's Wake/Lamplighter; The Ash Grove; Prince William; The German Beau; Mount Cashel's

Brigade; Kitty McGee (with bagpipes and french horn); Reel de Jeanne Marie; DeMartelly; Tell Her I Am; Scollay's Reel; Green Hills of Tyrol; Glenn Towle; Pipe On The Hop, and Piper's Lass.

Other outtakes retrieved from this period include cuts of Bobby Shafto/Simple Gifts; Cooley's Reel; Brisk Young Lads/2 and 6 Penny Girl; Prince William; Scotch Hornpipe, and Star Label Reel/Ned Kendall.

Swinging On A Gate, Canterbury Country Dance Orchestra

Recorded March 1974, Front Hall Records FHR-03

1.) Symondsbury/Mummer's March	3:10
2.) Lassies Fancy	3:24
3.) Dover Pier	3:33
4.) Johnny's Gone To France	1:18
5.) Rosebud Reel	2:28
6.) The False Bride, Kitty McGee	3:09
7.) Spanish Jig	3:24
8.) Bobby Shafto	3:43
9.) Dusty Bob Jig, Mouse In The Cupboard	3:36
10.) Still They Say She's Kind of Pretty (Dudley Laufman)	3:36
11.) All Around My Hat	3:43
12.) Fieldtown Processional	3:28
13.) Ring O'Bells	3:09
14.) Swinging On A Gate	3:47
15.) Zephyr & Flora	3:36

Musicians: Art Bryan, guitar; Peter Colby, banjo, autoharp; Dudley Laufman, accordion, harmonica, drum, bigotphone, tambourine, morris bells; April Limber, fiddle; Bob McQuillen, piano and accordion; Deanna Stiles, flute, piccolo.

Canterbury Folk at the Belknap Mill, Laconia NH
Cassette tape, recorded in the 1970s

1.) Low-Backed Car (jig)		2:42
2.) Bluebird Polka		2:43
3.) Ilka Moor		4:06
4.) Keel Row (schottische)		2:56
5.) Reel Pitou		2:16
6.) George Fox Monks March		3:27
7.) Streets of Laredo/Home On The Range (waltz)		3:07
8.) Nonesuch (polka)		2:33
9.) Quirk's Jig		2:14
10.) Drink To Me Only (waltz)		3:07
11.) Jig by Hayden/Jig by Handel		2:20
12.) The Keeper		2:18
13.) Tight Little Island (schottische)		3:30
14.) The Irish Girl (Richard Gehrts)		4:48

Musicians: Dudley and Patty Laufman, Barry and Gretchen Draper, and Richard Gehrts.

Shake A Leg, Canterbury Folk at the Marble Palace
New Hampshire Historical Society 1981 Andrea Records 10002

1.) The Sweets of May		3:13
2.) Goose's Minuet		3:09
3.) Lord of the Northern Sea		4:25
4.) Scattery Island Slide		2:44
5.) Woodland Dream (Bob McQuillen)		5:27
6.) Grandfather's Clock (Work)		2:16
7.) Black Joak		2:27
8.) The Road to the Isles (Macleod/Kennedy-Fraser/Nevell)		3:04
9.) White Mountains (Bob McQuillen)		3:03

10.) Clementine	3:45
11.) The Mozart (Laufman/Mozart)	2:26
12.) Farewell to the Creeks	2:10
13.) The Man in the Moon	3:45

Musicians: Lui Collins, vocals; Barry Draper, recorder; Carl Jacobs, bass; Dudley Laufman, accordion; Patty Laufman, vocals; Dick Nevell; Martha Wiederhold, vocals.

The Belle of the Contradance

Canterbury Country Dance Orchestra

F&W Records Recorded June 9, 1986. Cassette release (reissued on CD, 2016)

1.) The Holly Berry	3:28
2.) Planxty Fanny Power	4:15
3.) La Grondeuse II	3:30
4.) Sir Roger de Coverly/Drops of Brandy (medley)	2:19
5.) Lindbergh's Crate/ Green Cockade (medley)	3:15
6.) When I Grow Too Old To Dream (Sigmund Romberg)	3:42
7.) Jenny's Bawbee/Kafoozalem (medley)	2:39
8.) Piper's Lass/Lamplighter's Hornpipe (medley)	3:49
9.) Rye Waltz	3:43
10.) Lady Walpole's Reel	3:44
11.) Caber Feigh	3:22
12.) Gobby "O"	3:21
13.) Rope Waltz	3:24
14.) Constitution Hornpipe	3:52
15.) McQuillen's Squeezebox (Ralph Page)	3:29
16.) Pigtown Fling/Peter Street (medley)	3:53
17.) Belle of the Contradance (Greg Boardman)	6:40

Musicians: Greg Boardman, fiddle, guitar, vocal; Dave Fuller, accordion, harmonica; R.P. Hale, hammered dulcimer; Cal Howard, piano, bass; Randy Miller, fiddle; Allan McIntire, melodian, harmonica; Sylvia Miskoe, accordion; Dick Nevell, guitar; Lydia deAmicus Reeve, fiddle; Jack Sloanaker, piano, bass; Deanna M. Stiles, flute, piccolo; Jerry Weene, 5-string banjo, fiddle, mandolin; Taylor Whiteside, fiddle, viola, piano, balalaika; Dudley Laufman, accordion.

Where'd You Get Them Great Chunes?

Dudley Laufman, Jacqueline Laufman, and the Sugar River Band
Reels, Hornpipes, and a Jig, 2006

1.) Gloucestershire Hornpipe	3:13
2.) Honest John	2:59
3.) Trumpet Hornpipe	3:08
4.) Reel a Pitou	3:52
5.) Reel Joliette	3:11
6.) Christmas Hornpipe	3:15
7.) Waltz Quadrille	3:59
8.) Liberation (Siegal)	3:52
9.) Money Musk	2:54
10.) Princess Royal	3:24
11.) Opera Reel	3:39
12.) Larry's Waltz (Bob McQuillen)	7:01

Musicians: Dudley Laufman, fiddle and harmonica; Jacqueline Laufman, fiddle, with the Sugar River Band: Jane Orzechowski, fiddle; Francis Orzechowski, piano and accordion; Russell Orzechowski. fiddle; Sophie Orzechowski, fiddle, piano, and accordion; Neil Orzechowski, fiddle and limberjack; Larry Siegal, piano and mandolin.

Chocolate Soda
Dudley Laufman
Stories, Poems, and Tunes, 2006

1.) Plain Chocolate Soda   4:36
2.) Fern   0:43
3.) Dido, Bendigo   3:19
4.) In the Hammock   0:55
5.) Jacob   3:08
6.) Heron   3:18
7.) Longjohns   1:15
8.) Petronella   3:32
9.) Pig   1:25
10.) Shaker Ghosts   0:39
11.) All the Way to Galway   4:55
12.) Wood   1:56
13.) When We Go Into The Woods   2:50
14.) Gramps   1:52
15.) The Country Life (I Like To Rise)   2:09
16.) Strongbow   2:49
17.) World Turned Upside Down   3:24

Welcome Here Again
Canterbury Country Dance Orchestra
Recorded at the Middlesex School Chapel, Concord, MA
Sunday, March 20, 2016

1.) Welcome Here Again   3:44
2.) Come Up The Back Stairs   3:32
3.) Roxburgh Castle   3:57
4.) Moon & 7 Stars   3:03
5.) Charley Murray's Waltz (Jordan Tirrell-Wysocki)   5:25

6.) Marlboro Street (Dudley Laufman)   3:42

7.) Connacht Man's Rambles   2:58

8.) Cotillion des Baies-des-Rochers   3:52

9.) Blackberry Quadrille   3:11

10.) Forester's Hornpipe   3:08

11.) Monk's March   3:12

12.) The Waterloo Dance   4:51

13.) Rory O'More   3:52

14.) Sweet Richard   4:04

15.) Scotty O'Neil (Bob McQuillen)   3:43

16.) Colonel Robertson   4:58

17.) Constancy   3:50

18.) Buckwheat Batter   3:42

19.) My Love Is But A Lassie Yet   3:51

20.) Reprise: Charley Murray's Waltz (Tirell-Wysocki) 1:09

Musicians: Dudley Laufman, melodion and harmonica; Greg Boardman, fiddle; Art Bryan, banjo and guitar; Carl Jacobs, bass; Jacqueline Laufman, fiddle, Allan McIntyre, accordion; Sylvia Miskoe, accordion; Vince O'Donnell, fiddle; Jane Orzechowski, fiddle; Sadie Orzechowski, fiddle; Neil Orzechowski, fiddle; Russell Orzechowski, piano; Jack Perron, fiddle and mandolin; Wally Sweet, flute; Jordan Tyrell-Wysocki, fiddle; Taylor Whiteside, fiddle and guitar. Recording engineer, Gerry Putnam of Cedarhouse Studios, Sutton, NH.

Here's to Every Country Dancer

Canterbury Country Dance Orchestra
Recorded at Wind In the Timothy, Shaker Road, Canterbury, NH. Sunday, April 7, 2019. All tunes except Waltz Inverness composed by Dudley Laufman.

1.) Tara's Reel   3:08

2.) Mistwold   6:06

3.) Jig in A	3:05
4.) Waltz Inverness	3:14
5.) Hunting Song	2:54
6.) Burly Ivy	3:04
7.) Schottische for the First Day of Spring	4:47
8.) Fallen Leaves	3:45
9.) Patty's Orange Cape	3:46
10.) Glenn Towle	7:33
11.) Blue Joak	2:33
12.) Ballad for Edward Thomas	2:48
13.) Dave Fuller	3:15
14.) Inga's Birthday	3:12
15.) DeMartelly	3:34
16.) Little Girl Under The Stairs	2:00
17.) The Mozart	3:26
18.) Still They Say She's Kinda Pretty	3:05
19.) Waltz Inverness	2:37
20.) Marlborough Street	3:03

Musicians: Dudley Laufman, melodion, harmonica, fiddle, and vocals; Greg Boardman, fiddle; Art Bryan, banjo; Tom Curren, guitar and vocal; Lindsay Holden, fiddle and vocal; Sue Hunt, piano and accordion; Sylvia Miskoe, accordion; Jane Orzechowski, fiddle; Russell Orzechowski, fiddle, piano; Gerry Putnam, vocal; Walt Sweet, fife, flute; Bill Zecker, bass. Recording engineer, Gerry Putnam, Cedarhouse Studios, Sutton, NH.

Extensive collections of Dudley Laufman's music and writing are archived at the University of New Hampshire, at the University of Massachusetts, and at the New Hampshire Historical Society.

Index

Acknowledgements

THANK YOU, DUDLEY, for entrusting this light to me. And thanks to you and Nanci Aguair for allowing me to interrupt Thursday mornings during the busiest time of the young year on Shaker Road. Thanks to my partner Kathy Neustadt, for her love, her tolerance, and her support. Thanks to Greg Boardman, Art Bryan, Ted Levin, Sylvia Miskoe, and Vince O'Donnell, who have kindly and freely shared their thoughts with me, as, over the years, have other members of the Canterbury Country Dance Orchestra and other folks who count themselves as part of the New Hampshire community. Thanks to Rose Donnelley, Mary Lyn Ray, Ron Cameron, Richard Nylander, Gerry Putnam, Syd Lea, Geoff Muldaur, and Phil Ginsburg for believing in this book's promise. Thanks to Deidre Randall of Peter E. Randall Publisher for being there every step of the way, and to Lissa Warren for her skill and her energy. Thanks to David Mallett, Mary Dellea, and Robert Frost for borrowing their phrases "the summers of our dreams," "the towns that know us well," and the region that will "always take us in when we have no place to go" at the close of the piece. Thanks to Frank and Phoebe Griswold for taking Kathy and me in when we had nowhere to go, and for giving us a solid roof over our heads and a stout old cellar under us to support this work and to sustain our lives.

Thanks to everyone, everywhere, who continues to keep the faith. I've only been able to speak with a small fraction of you, under the circumstances, yet I hope that I have sufficiently honored the traditions you continue to love and care for.

*"Most of us around here have been dancing long
enough this time around to have gotten into some
of the more complicated contras like Money Musk,
Petronella, Chorus Jig, Rory O'More, and the like. But
only a few years ago we were all beginners and had to
learn from scratch. The contra dance is a lost art except
in a few parts of New Hampshire, Vermont, and
Maine, where, somehow, someway, it has been kept
alive in one form or another. But for many people it
is a skill that must be re-learned. Like house building
or growing your own food.... For the time being I'd
rather see you cut your teeth on the simpler dances and
sort of get your sea legs under you. It's like skating, you
know—you don't learn how to do it and play hockey
in the same day."*

—*Dudley Laufman*

About the Author

Tom Curren is a writer, farmer, conservationist, and historian who lives in rural New Hampshire with his wife, folklorist Kathy Neustadt. As project director with the Pew Charitable Trusts and as director of local conservation organizations, Tom has helped enable the conservation of nearly 900,000 acres in New England, New York, and Pennsylvania's Amish country. He has served as a town selectman, a town moderator, and non-profit volunteer and consultant.

Since the 1970s, Tom has written and spoken publicly about New England culture and landscape. He has published four town histories as well as the statewide account of Old Home Day. He has given talks at dozens of historical gatherings, and as part of the singing group "The Good Old Plough" he has appeared at dozens of locations, including the Shelburne Museum and Canterbury Shaker Village, as well as on NBC's Good Morning America and in televised performances on public radio and television.

Tom recently published a history of the Boston-Cambridge Folk Revival titled *I Believe I'll Go Back Home*, which *Library Journal* reviewed as follows: "Curren's work is both historically important and vital reading for the present moment. Our need for a spiritual and cultural revival is, it would seem, as essential and natural as our need to sing…Ultimately, the book is about America writ large, the power of our best (and worst) selves, and the role of music in inspiring, reflecting, and recovering the ideals of various times and people. In this time of discord, Curren hits exactly the right note."

Tom continues to play and sing traditional music (at times with Dudley Laufman and friends), to volunteer for the Folk New England Archive at the University of Massachusetts, and to speak and write in the service of remembrance and redemption throughout the region. He is completing an appreciation of the New England Village period between 1780 and 1830, a book project he postponed in order to complete *All Join Hands*.